D1194971

The Grey Zone

Ansvarig utgivare: Michaela Ahlberg and Anna Romberg
Framställd av Vulkan.se, tryckt i Riga

ISBN 978-91-639-7883-8

The Grey Zone

A PRACTICAL GUIDE
TO CORPORATE CONDUCT,
COMPLIANCE AND BUSINESS ETHICS

MICHAELA AHLBERG and ANNA ROMBERG

Content

Chapter ONE   Corporate conduct – why it matters 5

Chapter TWO   **Corporate Conduct – Expectations and Drivers for Change** 10

Drivers of Change 12
Lawful today – Questionable tomorrow 18
The United Nations' View 21

Chapter THREE   **From Words to Action, From Action to Change – a framework for managing corporate conduct** . . 25

An Overview of the Framework 26
One Costume, Different Sizes 32

Chapter FOUR   **Understand your Context and Content** 34

Risks from How We Behave – Conduct Risks. 37
A Model for Conduct Risk Assessment. 39
Your Company – Your Content 58

Chapter FIVE   **Compliance – from Words to Action** 62

Risk Assessment 64
Organisation. 70
Policies and Procedures. 79
Training and Communication 87
Speaking Up and Investigations 98
Remediation, disciplinary and corrective actions. 116
Third parties. 123
Reporting and Improvement 141
Oversight, monitoring and governance. 149

Chapter SIX   **Conduct and Culture – From Action to Change**. . 158

Leadership and the real "tone from the top" 159
Friction as a driver for change. 163
Culture is what you do – in the grey zone! 177

CHAPTER ONE

Corporate conduct – why it matters

In our transparent and global society, companies and their leaders are increasingly challenged on corporate conduct, on how they do business and on the consequences of their decisions. We follow corporate scandals as they unfold in newspapers and other media and there seem to be a never-ending stream of illegal and unethical business practices being revealed. The scandals not only lead to a tarnished reputation and legal consequences for the company but also have consequences for senior managers when, as a response to criticism, one of them is chosen as the "fall guy" and forced to leave. The scandals also have financial impact beyond the company itself as the share price may plunge drastically. Scandals frequently involve bribes paid through agents, fraud conducted by previously trusted managers and money funnelled through complex owner-ship structures to offshore accounts. Sweatshops with children and grownups working under what can only be described as slave-like conditions. Leaders taking advantage of positions of power, making sexual advances, lewd and improper "jokes" and various acts of discrimination. Sales activities and business entertainment in strip clubs or with escort services. Adding harassment and bullying of employees who speak up, ignoring unacceptable behaviour and even violence, companies are put to shame and struggle to explain how they ended up in this situation and how they plan to cred-ibly deal with these challenges. Companies, not yet exposed for wrongdoing fear reading about themselves in the headlines and try to learn from the mistakes of others. The companies, their board of directors and their management have plenty of statements fine-tuned by the communications department as everyone wants to "do the right thing". But how are these words put into action and is the action leading to real and lasting change? Dedication and competence in business ethics, compliance and managing corporate conduct, not only keeps companies out of trouble but also protects shareholder value, creates healthier organisations, enables business opportunities and can be a competitive advantage over time.

Despite the ever-increasing pace of the corporate world, it is surprising to see the lagging change in corporate conduct. A recent survey[1] indicates that more than one-third of employees see a conflict between their company's corporate values and the way in which business actually is conducted. The same survey shows that three out of ten were worried about negative consequences for themselves personally if they raised concerns, and one in five have seen people turning a blind eye to inappropriate behaviour. Another survey[2] indicates that one-third of directors and senior managers would justify offering cash payments to win business. Over 50 % of the respondents had information or concerns about misconduct in their organisation and almost half of these (48 %) had felt pressure to withhold this information, and more than half (56 %) chose not to report. When challenged about misconduct, research indicates[3] that companies spend more time and effort denying or refusing allegations of misconduct than actually doing something about it. Why these disappointing statistics? Why is there not a more visible impact from corporate statements and ambitions? We believe there is a will to change corporate behaviour, but is the way clear? We believe that achieving the right corporate conduct requires more than statements to "do the right thing" and relying on an assumption or aspiration of "good corporate culture". In the community of ethics and compliance professionals, there is

1   UK Banking Standards Board Annual Review 2016/2017.

2   EY Europe, Middle East, India and Africa fraud survey 2017.

3   Vandekerckhove, W, Leys, J. and Van Braeckel, D. (2007). That's not what happened and it's not my fault anyway! An exploration of management attitudes towards SRI-shareholder engagement. Business Ethics: a European Review, 16 (4), p. 403–418.

constant discussion about what is most important: culture or rules. We believe the simple answer is both. Determination, transparent discussions, consistent decisions and a systematic approach are required to manage corporate conduct. Lasting change and a culture of doing things right does not come about by itself. It requires actions that speak louder than words.

On the reception wall of the telecommunications company Moldcell in Moldavia, you can read, "We have a strategy. It's called getting things done". This is exactly what we aim for – to get things done – to put words into action and follow through to ensure that the action leads to lasting change. In this book, we will describe how

> "We have a strategy. It's called getting things done"

we have worked to address corporate conduct. We will explain how corporate culture is built through difficult decisions, priorities and frictions. We will also describe how implementation of a systematic ethics and compliance framework will feed and enable lasting change. Furthermore, we will describe why and how ethics and compliance as well as rules and culture are interdependent. We will draw from many years of experience working with various global companies. For three years, we worked together at Telia Company, a Swedish multinational company, subject to corruption investigations in several jurisdictions. During these years, we built an organisation and a framework for ethics and compliance in preparation for and anticipation of negotiations and settlement agreement with the US Department of Justice, US Stock Exchange Commission as well as Dutch and Swedish prosecutors. These years have been crucial for our understanding of how implementation of an ethics and compliance framework really works. Why it is important to "stick to the programme" and to be consistent: the framework is not a smorgasbord where you can pick and choose. We also learned that an effective compliance programme, through increased transparency and awareness, will result in frictions, struggles and will force dilemmas to the decision-making table. And we came to understand that corporate culture evolves, based on how these difficult discussions, conflicts and frictions are handled. We learned that ethics and compliance is ultimately a matter of brave and determined leadership, allowing for transparency and facilitating honest discussions around hard choices and dilemmas. Even if the work, to some extent, was difficult and exhausting, it was at the same time rewarding, in light of the recognition that the ethics and compliance programme received in dialogue with leaders and employees in the company as well as with regulators, shareholders and other stakeholders. In the final settlement, due to a deferred prosecution agreement with the authorities in the US and the Netherlands, the company received a full discount for the remediation and ethics and compliance work; moreover, due to the extensive remediation and state of the ethics and compliance work undertaken since end of 2013, a corporate monitor was not appointed. Since this endeavour, our work has continued in different corporate arenas and we have a firm belief that corporations play a crucial role in the development of our societies and environment. We believe that corporations can play a role where local governments have failed. We also believe that corporations can break patterns of normalised and silenced acceptance of misconduct. Furthermore, corporations can and should create value for their shareholders as well as for stakeholders within their full sphere of influence. However, there is room for improvement – there is room for improving corporate conduct.

This book is written for anyone who wants to explore the multifaceted landscape of corporate conduct. The first chapter lays the foundation of why corporate conduct matters. Chapter Two describes the increased expectations on corporations and some key drivers for change. Chapter Three provides an overview of the implementation framework for managing corporate conduct, a framework for putting words into action and going from action to change. Chapters Four and Five are mainly written as a handbook for professionals working or aspiring to work with ethics and compliance, corporate responsibility and with building responsible organisations. These chapters describe a practical implementation framework for putting words into action, a framework that is designed to meet regulatory requirements for effective ethics and compliance and adequate procedures. We have tested the framework in reality and believe it provides a benchmark for your own compliance programmes and will hopefully inspire development of your current way of working. Chapter Six explains what happens when words are put into action, a description for how real change requires leadership. To achieve change, one must also look at the compliance methodology as a tool to make dilemmas visible, enabling and empowering leaders to tackle them. Dilemmas are rarely black and white: different priorities and human factors add to the complexity creating a grey zone of right and wrong, a grey zone of possible decisions. Leaders must therefore learn to navigate this grey zone, embracing frictions and struggles and make decisions defining who they and their companies truly are.

Chapter TWO

Corporate Conduct – Expectations and Drivers for Change

Change is constant, something we all recognise. It is difficult to lead and change corporate strategies, directions, manners, processes and cultures and many management books deal with this leadership challenge. The challenge to understand and adopt lasting change also how business is done. Maybe it is even more difficult to follow and address *behavioral* change, the how, as we are talking about matters not directly related to the company's products, services or technology. Usually, strategy documents, business plans and leadership meetings focus on what the company is selling such as cars, fashion, telecommunication services, transportation or windmills and not on how the company (its employees, leaders, suppliers, agents and other third parties) conduct themselves.

The root cause of many sustainability-related challenges both societal and environmental, is often global systemic corruption and poor governance in developing and/or kleptocratic countries. In other words, the development aid paid to build schools ends up in corrupt officials' pockets. Public assets and tax money, which rightfully belong to the people, are channelled to secret offshore entities, with the ultimate benefit going to the ruling elite, enriching themselves at the expense of the local society and people. Environmental laws are circumvented and rivers are polluted because officials are bribed to issue an environmental certificate. The same goes for work and labour conditions, where bribery and corruption make it easy to buy required certificates and avoid or manipulate inspections. Children are forced to work because the local society is not developing, and international businesses may decide to stay away from markets because of a difficult, bureaucratic or unpredictable business environment. A global anticorruption survey from 2017, with more than 300 general counsel and compliance officers participating, suggested that corruption continues to be a major concern for businesses and that companies have increasingly stopped doing business with certain partners (42%, up from 32%) or lost business (31%, up from 23%) due to corruption risk[4]. Corruption distorts competition and makes businesses inefficient.

A study published by World Economic Forum indicates that firms operating in a highly corrupt environment are likely to employ a higher number of workers due to misallocation of talent and that employees may be engaged in unproductive activities such as searching for ways to circumvent bureaucratic constraints.[5] Sarah Chayes, the 2015 winner of Los Angeles Times Book Prize for Current Interest with her book "Thieves of State", makes a compelling argument that corruption is an insidious force, resulting in some of the most dangerous challenges that are facing the world and threatening global security.

But the major challenges with regards to corruption risk in the context of business can also be an opportunity as risk and opportunity always go hand in hand. By recognising and adapting to the change in society and the business environment, as well as new expectations and requirements for improved conduct, a company may be able find opportunities at the core of their business. These opportunities may relate to innovative solutions for sustainable business or lead to a more attractive workplace. The opportunities may also enable a company to engage in profitable business in challenging contexts, such as in countries with corrupt systems; thus, by doing so, the company is not only reaping profits but also contributing to a stronger business environment on a global scale.

---

4   https://www.alixpartners.com/insights-impact/insights/2017-global-anticorruption-survey-lost-business-dissolved-partnerships-and-data-s-critical-role/

5   https://www.weforum.org/agenda/2015/05/how-does-corruption-affect-economic-growth/

Drivers of Change

Today's most experienced business and sales managers have to a large extent been fostered in a business climate that is different from the one we have today. It was a climate where extravagant skiing trips paid for by the suppliers were acceptable, where you ensured that your relatives and friends got the best jobs and where local "challenges" were solved by hiring a consultant to "get things done". It was perhaps even a climate where bribes were tax deductible as legitimate "cost of doing business"; in 1996 only 14 OECD countries denied the deductibility of bribes to foreign public officials as a general rule[6]. Today, several factors put pressure on companies and their leaders to challenge and rethink how business has been and is done.

From Limited Transparency to Hyper Transparency

Gone are the days when companies could separate internal and external communication. Information and news travel at light speed. If you are not open, you run a big risk that someone else will be and you will end up in an uphill struggle for trust and credibility. The US Department of Justice (DOJ) and the UK Serious Fraud Office (SFO) are monitoring media and are also only a phone call away offering financial incentives for people to blow the whistle.[7] Considering that managements and boards have several different stakeholders to make allowances for, increased transparency may be the only reasonable way forward to explain the different and sometimes opposing priorities and interests that these

---

6   http://oecdobserver.org/news/archivestory.php/aid/245/Writing_off_tax_deductibility_.html

7   The Dodd-Frank Act in the US requires the Securities and Exchange Commission (SEC) to reward whistle-blowers who voluntarily provide original information regarding securities violations or bribes paid to foreign officials in violation of the Foreign Corrupt Practices Act (FCPA). Section 922 of the law awards whistle-blowers 10 to 30 per cent of any monetary recovery of over $1 million that the SEC obtains from an offending party through enforcement actions. There are law firms specialising in supporting reporters, ensuring that they will maximise their reward.

stakeholders may hold. It is tempting to sugarcoat information, or at least limit the negative information and focus on positive news and praise for good behaviour and accomplishments. This is human behaviour and we admit to it ourselves, but the best crisis management tool is being transparent. Do not just report on your accomplishments; report on your struggles, failures and challenges. It is much wiser to talk about the improvements needed yourself than wait until the media highlights your weaknesses.

It is only through honest transparency that you can buy yourself the time required to build trust.

Transparency is especially helpful when trust is gone or worn thin. Transparency is the only way forwards to build trust even if it is a bitter pill to swallow. When it comes to corporate conduct, the road from words to action is not straightforward but winding, narrow and full of bumps and detours, so we may as well be honest from the outset.

From Indifference to Distrust

Corporate scandals/crises are common; we read and hear about them daily in the media. Globalisation and hyper-transparency enables us to follow, more or less hour by hour, as the crisis unfolds. Corporate scandals contribute to an all-time low of trust in businesses and business leaders, as we can see from Edelman's 2018 Trust Barometer.[8]

---

8   https://www.edelman.com/trust2018/

Top 10 Reasons for Distrust in Business (UK)	General population	Youth
Top executives are overpaid compared to the average worker	58 %	42 %
They do not pay their fare share of tax	56 %	50 %
They do not operate in a transparent and honest way	45 %	38 %
Corruption is commonly accepted	42 %	37 %
The average worker is mistreated or taken advantage of	42 %	43 %
They do not communicate honestly when problems arise	40 %	32 %
They do not play a role in giving back to the communities in which they operate	33 %	34 %
They fight to weaken regulations that protect average people	31 %	30 %
They do not take a stand on issues that matter to society	28 %	33 %
They do not keep people's data and personal information safe	27 %	22 %

source: 2018 Edelman Trust Barometer UK supplement

The corporate scandals/crises and awareness of shrinking trust in corporate leaders (and possibly in combination with the ever shrinking trust in politicians and governance of the states, i.e. "the system") compels corporate leaders to step up. Step up to address their stakeholders' damaged trust in them and the company they represent but also increasingly, to show a willingness to assume responsibility for how their business operations can contribute to a more sustainable world. Corporations are expected to show that they deserve the trust they have been given by more than just words.

From Local to Global - Interdependency

Very few companies today are truly local. At the very least, a local company may have suppliers and service providers that are not. We are all part of a global web and structure and are interdependent on each other, across artificial barriers such as borders, walls and nationality. Therefore, understanding corporate conduct risks is quite an effort, as analysing and understanding only local laws, local stakeholders, local expectations and requirements is not enough. One country after another introduces legislation that reaches outside their own country; amongst the most famous are the US Foreign Corrupt Practices Act (US FCPA), the UK Bribery Act (UKBA), the French Sapin II Anti-corruption law and regulations on discrimination and labour rights including the recent UK Modern Slavery Act and Tax Evasion Act. All are examples of extraterritorial legislation that a company may unknowingly be subject to. There are also increasing requirements and expectations that a company is responsible for not only its own actions but also for those of its suppliers, vendors, agents, distributors and partners – sometimes these expectations are codified in legislation and sometimes they are expectations of ethical business practices. Pictures of terrible working conditions or details of dubious business parties spread like wildfire as regulators share information and non-governmental organisations work across borders. Corporate conduct cannot be contained locally but needs to live up to global standards.

From Shareholder Value to Significant Stakeholders

"The company" is often and historically translated to "the [current] shareholders". However, companies today are increasingly expected to also assume responsibility towards society, environment and human rights as well as its global footprint and impact on future generations. Companies have to establish who the important stakeholders of the company are. The Board's fiduciary duty towards the shareholders, who have put them there to protect their interests, does not necessarily preclude them from considering other significant stakeholder interests. In the Statement of Significant Audiences and Materiality[9], it is suggested that the board can identify specific stakeholders of materiality and their own commitments towards such stakeholders. The statement not only ensures

---

9   Eccles, R. G. and Youmans, T. Materiality in Corporate Governance: The Statement of Significant Audiences and Materiality. Journal of Applied Corporate Finance, (2016) 28: 39–46.

transparency of responsibilities and commitments but also, more importantly, opens the door to a more intelligent and transparent conversation between the company and the stakeholders on the priorities and difficulties the management and company will go through in making choices when different interests collide.

From Lawyer to Advocate

Some lawyers have found that being a corporate lawyer has, from time to time, required them to "think creatively", "find workarounds", "get the deal done" or "stop being a nay-sayer", leaving them with a sense that they are themselves a supporter and enabler of unethical and maybe even ultimately unlawful business transactions. In a changing world, modern lawyers understand that the job also requires them to be an advocate of interests other than short-term profits and to consider other stakeholders than the immediate boss. The role of the corporate lawyer or general counsel is to give the decision makers relevant and current information, not only on legal risks but also on ethical expectation risks, societal risks and reputational risk such as explaining that the management and the board might have to consider the wider implications from a certain business arrangement. The days when a formal agreement and an anti-corruption clause could protect the company are over. Nowadays, lawyers are expected to know better, to understand inferences and red flags and to act in the long-term interest of the company and its stakeholders.

We argue that ethics and compliance cannot be separated and that understanding this is fundamental. The concept of ethics and compliance is rather new or unknown to many people working outside the US business context. Many wonder if it is a function or description of a working methodology. Is it maybe a "layer of defence" or control mechanism? Is ethics part of compliance or can they be separated, so compliance is one thing (legal compliance) and ethics another (more voluntary part)? There are different opinions on these questions, but our view is that ethics and compliance are both a function and a model/methodology for ensuring that what the leaders say also happens throughout the organisation. We believe that compliance cannot be separated from ethics. Ethics is not an extra layer of protection on top of legal requirements or an "impact cushion" or to be considered as a margin in the corporate rules framework and when ending up in difficult situations, challenging both these rules and your own good sense by asking for a "legal" opinion. Instead, you should ask for advice and opinions about legal, ethical, reputational and societal risks.

Instead of asking for a legal opinion, ask for advice and opinions about legal, ethical, reputational and societal risks.

Ethics is the foundation of legislation; it is our common view of right and wrong, where legislation is the formalised interpretation. Ethical awareness is strengthened by an understanding of why legislation is needed and a broader sense of the responsibilities and risks involved. Ethical awareness enables you to have a better grasp of the intentions as well as the limitations of the law. With stronger ethical awareness, we can also understand how and why laws may change over time, as people get smarter in circumventing them and the societal expectations change. Ethics should really be a mandatory part of the curriculum in business schools and legal education, to ensure that new aspirational leaders and lawyers avoid the misconception that ethics is a luxury, an extra layer of good behaviour, when instead it is an intricate part of day-to-day business practice.

From Black or White to The Grey Zone

As described in the previous section, legal and compliance professionals have certainly and repeatedly been asked: "just tell us what we can do", "just tell us how this can be legally done", "just help us to get the paperwork right". But rarely is legislation black or white and neither is global business. For example a company that is not directly subject to the US sanctions regime may be able to complete certain sales transactions within the legal boundaries. Nevertheless, by selling to a party that is sanctioned the company may disappoint ethical expectations and be presented in a very bad light in the media and may, as a consequence, even be barred from funding by, for example, the World Bank or IMF. Global business is about navigating the grey zone, which is not so much a driver for change, but a consequence of increased awareness of different stakeholder interests, a complex legal landscape of changed requirements and expectations. Business leaders are constantly faced with difficult decisions where circumstances are rarely black or white. Leaders must be empowered to navigate the grey zone.

Lawful today – Questionable tomorrow

Companies also need to understand that what is done today has to stand up to scrutiny over time. What is legal today may be illegal tomorrow.

- In 2008, Siemens paid a record 1.6 billion USD in legal settlements in the US and Europe following a bribery scandal, where bribes paid over the years, had gone from deductibles in the German tax returns to morally and ethically deplorable acts as well as being illegal. The settlement documents detail systematic and deliberate bribery since the mid-1990s as well as systematic efforts to falsify corporate books and records and knowingly failing to implement and circumvent existing internal controls.

- In 2011 the US retail giant Walmart self-reported possible bribes in Mexico, Brazil, China and India. In May 2018 the company had spent more than 877 MUSD on legal defences and internal compliance measures as well as reserved 283 MUSD for anticipated fines. This equals to approximately 530,000 USD spent each day since 2012.

- In 2013, the Rana Plaza building in Dhaka Bangladesh collapsed, killing over a thousand garment workers, injuring many more and sending shock waves across the world as the deadliest garment factory accident in history. The factory owner had run a business without consideration for health, safety or labour rights of the factory workers, and among the customers were big international brands worn by many of us. Questions remain as to how the building ever met the quality standards applicable for factories; perhaps an official was bribed to issue the necessary permits?

- In 2016, the Swedish business elite realised that public opinion did not condone expensive business entertainment, such as using corporate private jets for executives, their families and pets or excessive mixing of business and pleasure. A painful realisation for some individuals who lost their executive and board positions and tarnished their reputation. Although assured that no illegality had taken place, they became aware that ethics and morals mattered more to the general public.

- In 2017, Telia Company announced that they would pay 965 MUSD to settle a bribery investigation with the Dutch and US authorities. The corrupt activity and bribery went back to 2007 when the company decided to establish a business operations in Uzbekistan. In 2008, the Swedish daily newspaper, Svenska Dagbladet, published an article questioning the lack of due diligence of the minority shareholder in the Uzbek joint venture and possible involvement of the corrupt regime. The CEO Lars Nyberg answered, "Even if I know the formal owner, I don't know who the beneficial owner is. Does it matter?". Surprisingly, there were very limited reactions to this article. In 2012, the very same information was published in the TV programme Uppdrag Granskning and triggered a scandal of unprecedented proportions as well as criminal investigations in three jurisdictions.

"What is perceived to be right and what is acceptable also changes over time. This makes it even more important that our acts can be justified from a moral and ethical standpoint. We, like many others, are to consider not only the rules and regulations of today, we always have to use our own ethical compass to explain and justify our positions at any point in the future".

(TeliaSonera transcript the chairman of the board's speech, AGM, 3 April 2013)

The United Nations' View

There are two important global frameworks to refer to when talking about expectations of corporate conduct: the 10 principles of the UN Global Compact on how business is carried out and the UN Sustainable Development Goals (SDG) on what the companies should strive for in relation to society, the environment and human rights.

UN Global Compact 10 Principles - HOW

"I propose that you, business leaders gathered in Davos, and we, the United Nations, initiate a global compact of shared values and principles, which will give a human face to the global market".

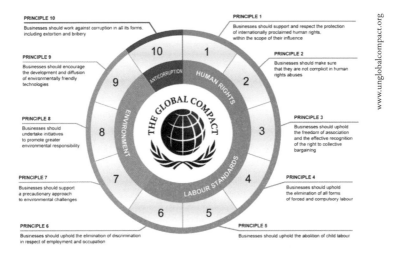

This statement was made by Kofi Annan in Davos 1999, when UN Global Compact and its principles on Human Rights, Labour practices and Environment was founded. The principles were complemented in 2004 with a principle relating to Anti-Bribery Corruption.

The ten principles of the UN Global Compact establish that corporations are responsible for how their business is carried out in relation to society, human rights and the environment. The principles are based on shared universal values that have been defined in international agreements such as the UN Universal Declaration of Human Rights, ILO Declaration on Fundamental Principles and Rights at Work and the Rio Declaration on Environment and Development. We think that understanding these universal and common values is really important and relevant, not just for politicians and public servants but also for corporations. These universal and common values came first and then the principles – much in the same way as we propose that common and shared values and ethics guide and drive rules and regulations.

Over 12,000 companies in more than 160 countries[10] have pledged their commitment under the UN Global Compact principles and committed to implement them in practice. What many are yet to realise is that the implementation requires substantial and persistent effort – and a humble attitude towards the related challenges. In general, the ten principles lay a foundation for what the ethics and compliance work should address and set the expectations for corporate conduct.

In 2008, the UN adopted a guiding framework, proposed by UN Special Representative John Ruggie, on businesses and human rights, called "Protect, Respect and Remedy". The framework describes the government's responsibility to protect and the corporation's responsibility to respect human rights as well as the joint responsibility of both parties to establish channels for reporting breaches and effective remedies to those affected in the event of those breaches against human rights. Today, we increasingly see companies conducting human rights impact assessments to understand what the company's responsibility really entails.

---

10   https://www.unglobalcompact.org/what-is-gc/participants

*"We don't have a plan B
because there is no planet B"*

General Ban Ki-moon

www.sustainabledevelopment.un.org

In 2015, the UN and UN Global Compact launched the UN Sustainable Development Goals (SDG). Seventeen goals to encourage and support businesses throughout the world to take strategic action to advance the worldwide common agenda to end poverty and hunger, improve health and education, make cities more sustainable, combat climate change, and protect oceans and forests.

The SDG are a great tool for demonstrating the kind of issues our planet is struggling with and to highlight the fact that solutions to these global problems will not come from politicians and governments. To reach the SDG, engagement, drive, leadership and innovation from companies are prerequisites. During the last year, there has been intense focus on the SDG, and many corporations worldwide signed up to the SDG and formulated a strategy with products and services that support one or several of the SDG. Innovation and dedication bring life to one admirable company after another, where the entire business idea and purpose supports the SDG and a better world in some way while still keeping a healthy profit.

In the midst of the SDG excitement, it may be easy to forget that companies committed to the SDG have also committed to the Global Compact principles. These ten principles require companies to work in a certain way and to ensure compliance throughout the value and supply chain. We argue that a company must have equal focus on both the Global Compact principles, representing how business is carried out and the SDG, representing what the company should strive to achieve. In the eyes of a businessperson, it may be more tempting to focus on the SDG as these revolve around business, innovation and opportunities. However, if companies are not complying with fundamental principles on human and labour rights, anti-corruption and environmental concerns the innovations will not solve the root cause of the problems that the SDG address.

Chapter THREE

From Words to Action, From Action to Change – a framework for managing corporate conduct

The framework that we have developed addresses how business is done. Not *what* a company is doing but *how* the company is taking responsibility for its actions and the consequences of its business. More specifically, as a corporation is a legal entity and therefore not capable of thought, decisions or actions, how the individuals, employees, agents and suppliers representing the legal entity are behaving. We talk about how the company is behaving in relation to society, the environment and human rights, and how the company, by its actions and inactions, is contributing, or not, to a sustainable future. We talk about the daily decisions and the difficult decisions. Is a decision-maker capable of saying no to a lucrative business deal if it entails using a questionable agent or consultant? How will the company react to and address the fact that a senior manager is harassing or silencing colleagues and employees, who have raised concerns. What we do as employees and leaders usually gets measured, rewarded and reported continuously. What we do is also mainly what the governance and internal control systems manage. What we do dominates the quarterly and annual reports. How we do things, how we conduct ourselves may not be an issue … until it is.

> How things are done is not perceived as an issue …until it is.

An Overview of the Framework

Our framework for managing corporate conduct, designed for moving "From Words to Action and From Action to Change", is based on the five fundamental Cs: Context, Content, Compliance, Conduct and Culture.

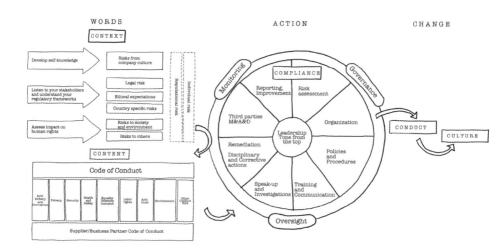

All of the elements, Context, Content, Compliance, Conduct and Culture, are required to truly address and manage corporate conduct. It takes two seconds to say "zero tolerance against corruption", and it is relatively easy to use words in annual reports and sustainability reports or in public speeches, to describe how responsible and sustainable the company aspires to be. Corporate scandals may reveal that the reality is something different and that the words have not been put into action. Effective compliance work is fundamental to living up to the words and generating action throughout the entire company.

Compliance brings transparency, makes difficult dilemmas visible and generates friction. The friction and dilemmas require decisions and actions, a conduct. And conduct demonstrated throughout the company will inevitably generate a culture. Words do not create culture, action does.

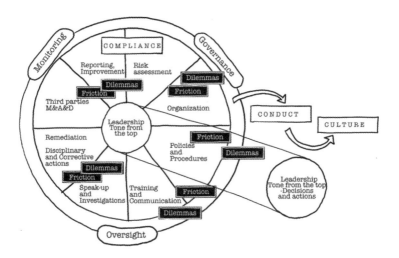

With time, and provided that the culture that has been built is based on transparent dialogue and responsible decisions, the culture of good business ethics will become stronger and the dilemmas generated from compliance work will be easier to solve, the friction easier to handle. If, on the other hand, dilemmas are not solved but pushed back into the compliance organisation or solved without taking into consideration commitment to the wider responsibility of the company, the friction will become difficult to manage. The compliance work will suffer and deteriorate; accordingly, the company will fail in its aspiration to manage corporate conduct in a responsible and ethical way. Lack of transparency and conflict between words and action (statements such as "we treat everyone equally" – but in reality only white males are promoted, or "we have zero tolerance for corruption" – but in reality acceptance of a "factory visit", which includes sightseeing, pocket money and personal recreation for executives at an important customer is common) will not only undermine efforts to build the culture, it will also create unbearable pressure on the compliance function and expose the company not only to the risk of an ethical breakdown but also legal and reputational risks. The compliance work will be ineffective. Many people refer to this as a "paper programme" or a "tick-in-the-box programme", which runs the risk of failing to protect the company when gaps between the words and action are revealed.

In a perfect world, a company would be able to start from understanding its context and then work onwards with content and compliance, conduct and culture. We realise that hardly any company starts with this work from scratch, and one has to adapt to what already exists. This framework provides a methodology of elements, which should ultimately all be in place for managing corporate conduct and our view on what to expect during the implementation and continued work. It will help you plan the work, ensure its effectiveness, identify where there is room for improvement and perhaps understand why the work may feel overwhelming at times. Struggles and friction are a natural part of change and we encourage embracing them and using them as fuel for change. Based on our experience, the friction and the fray are actually evidence of the programme having an impact and that the journey towards change has started. All the hard work will pay off in the form of more responsible corporate conduct and a stronger culture of business ethics.

The framework for managing corporate conduct starts with understanding the *Context* – the operational and legal environment, the expectations from sharehold-

ers and the impact the business has on the external environment.

By understanding and assessing the context, the company will be able to define the *Content*; specifically which aspects of behaviour and corporate conduct are most relevant for the company to systematically address. Are they concerned about price fixing or leakage of market sensitive information? Are they particularly

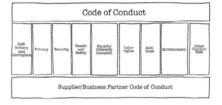

exposed to bribery and corruption or should they be more concerned about discrimination, diversity and inclusion? Or maybe the privacy of customer data or labour rights in the supply chain?

Compliance

The *Compliance* element describes the implementation of aspired conduct into actual conduct. A sincere and dedicated effort to implement change will inevitably require transparent, tough choices. Uncomfortable and difficult discussions may arise when conflicting priorities have to be addressed. How much should we invest in a system to manage customer data in times of financial austerity? Should we say no to this business deal as we know that it will involve a consultancy payment to an offshore tax haven? Should we ignore the possibility that a sales intermediary will share price information from one of our competitors with us? Do I have to fire my brilliant colleague because he is groping the female associates? Is this the tip of the iceberg or is it a random incident? Can I avoid an uncomfortable choice by ignoring it? These may not be clear-cut, easy, black or white choices but are oftentimes choices which have to be made in the grey zone and will require navigating in waters of uncertainty with conflicting priorities and different loyalties.

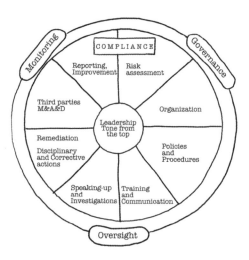

Conduct and Culture

How managers and leaders *Conduct* themselves and decide in these situations will, at the end of the day, build the *Culture*. Many companies claim that they have a "good corporate culture", "Nordic values", or "strong leadership", which automatically suggests that the employees "do things right". We argue that the culture, values and leadership are only as strong as the daily decisions, and that action speak louder than words. It does not matter how many people have been trained in areas of corporate conduct and that well-written policies exist if the leadership and decisions their undermine these efforts.

We will dig into each element, in more detail in chapters 4, 5 and 6 below.

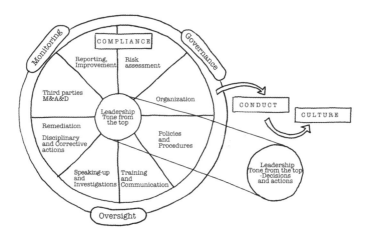

One Costume, Different Sizes

In this book we describe the framework for putting words into action and ensuring that the action results in true change, based on our experiences, lessons learned and conclusions. We have also used the experiences of friends and colleagues working at other companies. Working in ethics and compliance can sometimes be a lonely and difficult task so the professional community is active and important for sharing of experiences and advice as we all face more or less the same challenges. The companies we, and our professional peers, work for are very different. Some have a history of crises and regulatory enforcement, some have implemented a Code of Conduct but never reflected on the actual impact, some are global companies, some are local, some are headquartered in the Nordics and some in Dubai, London, New York or Singapore. Some companies are big stock-listed companies and some are small, family owned businesses. Some companies have big regulatory compliance departments (like banks) with years of experience in regulatory compliance, and some are starting their journey with their first Code of Conduct.

The most relevant risks for corporate misconduct will be different for each company, depending on the external and internal context. If you are in the forest industry, then environmental responsibility is probably high on the agenda. If you are in the fashion industry using many suppliers in Asia, then labour practices might be high on the agenda. If you do business in countries with high levels of kleptocracy or other forms of corruption, then that topic will be high on the agenda. If you are working in a bank, then the topic is understanding the source of the money flowing through the bank, as a critical step in the fight against global crime and corruption. Following the #metoo movement, it would seem as if diversity, inclusion and harassment should be a priority across all countries and industries. Regardless of which risks your company is exposed to, the framework of how to put words into action and action into change is the same and can be used by all businesses irrespective of size, operating model or industry. In analysing the requirements of ethics and compliance in regulations, which incidentally are on the rise globally, we see substantially the same cornerstones defining effective compliance (or adequate procedures). The framework for managing corporate conduct, for putting words into action and action into change, is not only the same for different businesses and different sizes of businesses but also applicable for businesses of different origins.

We wrote this book to address corporate conduct based on our experiences working in corporations funded by shareholders. However, the framework for managing corporate conduct could just as well be described as managing organisational conduct and applied in organisations funded by donors (NGOs) or by taxpayers (counties, municipalities, governments) as well as within organisations such as the UN. The context and content will be as unique as any company or organisation but the compliance methodology is the same.

So, we believe the costume is the same but, of course, the size must be different, depending on the relevant factors in each specific company and organisation.

We have come to understand that true change will not come out of fear, such as fear of legal proceedings, media exposure and personal disgrace. True change will only come from a desire to do what is right. Even if we talk a fair bit about legal consequences and reputational damage, it should not be the main driver for the work – the driver has to be a true desire to do what is right and understanding why this matters in the long run.

Chapter FOUR

Understand your Context and Content

When you start working with corporate conduct, it is fundamental to understand where you are and who you are. With this, we mean to understand both your external and internal context. Knowledge about the external environment and internal structures is key to making informed decisions and being able to structure the operations and processes in a relevant and responsible way. Is the external context entrenched in corruption? Is your industry exposed to scrutiny from regulatory authorities? Do your company operations, for example factories, have a negative impact on local societies and the environment? Is your organisation diverse and inclusive? Does your company have standardised and global business processes? Do your emplyees have good knowledge of the Code of Conduct and your underlying rules? Do they know where to turn if they have questions? Is the corporate culture transparent, allowing for discussion of dilemmas?

Do you know the answer to these questions or are you guessing?

When perception can be misleading

Transparency International publishes a Corruption Perception Index every year. The Nordic countries are always ranked highly, as the least corrupt countries in the world. Yet, Nordic companies, operating globally, have not been spared from scandals of corrupt business practices. Telia Company, a company with great history and partly owned by the Swedish and Finnish states, recently paid one of the largest amounts in fines and disgorgement for corruption offences to the US and Dutch authorities. Even the Swedish royal institution Svenska Akademien is facing an "annus horribilis" with allegations of corruption, harassment, retaliation and sexism resulting in a massive loss of trust in the institution itself and a decision not to issue a Nobel prize in literature for 2018. And then we have the Nordic banks, which are accused of and subsequently invstigated for the laundering of dirty money.

Many say that Nordic people have great values, which guide them when doing business. So, how is this possible with gross corruption offences committed by companies from this region? Some claim that Nordic people are so honest that they become naïve and fall prey to "local practices". Some say that they are just as corrupt as anyone else when opportunity knocks on the door or when going abroad. Others explain that conflicts are something to be avoided at any cost in the Nordics, where everyone should agree and make joint decisions. In the Nordics we are used to strong institutions, with the government regulating and controlling what is right and what is wrong. We pay our taxes, and we do not bribe the police. But do we know what corruption is and how it works? Do we naively do global business with a mindset formed by trust and our home

www.transparency.org

market context? Are we trained on how to act in a society where there are weak institutions and where high-ranking government officials ask for bribes? Are we trained to deal with situations where lack of control is seen as an opportunity and where bending the rules is the norm until someone enforces the rules?

A poor understanding of the context may result in the company putting its future operations and reputation at stake. Relying on individuals being able to navigate a complex environment because they are "Nordic" can be detrimental and put unfair pressure and expectations on individuals. The misjudgement of the external context, and individuals' capabilities to navigate the context in the Eurasian market proved to be detrimental for Telia Company. Not only did the company have to focus considerable management attention on the matter and spend huge amounts of money on resolving the legal issues, it then in the end decided to withdraw from these markets.

The Board of Directors' decision to dispose of the operations in the region of Eurasia will transform TeliaSonera. On the one hand, the margins in the region have been high, and historically the growth has been fast. On the other hand, it has been problematic in many ways to operate in the region. In some markets, we have unknown co-owners and it is difficult to repatriate cash. This and other challenges in the region have required our attention and lots of resources. The decision to leave has given and will continue to give us focus, strength and energy to develop our operations in the Nordic and Baltic countries ... "

(TeliaSonera Annual Report, 2015 p.8)

Telia Company's decision to leave a corrupt and human rights obstructive market is unfortunately not unique. There are examples of Swedish construction companies withdrawing from Latin America and Russia, and several multinational companies are wary of the Indian market despite huge opportunities. As stated, we firmly believe that an enlightened and professionally run company should be able to navigate these difficult markets. However, the more difficult the external context, the more will be required to ensure the right corporate conduct. If you operate in highly corrupt and obstructive markets, you cannot assume that the same governance and control structures, as for a less challenging market such as for example Scandinavia, will do the job.

Ethics and compliance is not only about risks

I always feel a need to correct statements about ethics and compliance as a risk management exercise and as a mere formality. I work with ethics and compliance because the work presents an opportunity to do good business to earn credibility and trust from customers, employees, vendors, shareholders and other stakeholders (future and current). Ethics and compliance is about ensuring that we can win business deals fairly in challenging markets, thus, safeguarding shareholders' investment and ensuring long-term value creation. It is about creating value for the company but also creating value for others in the form of stronger and equal societies by, for example, protecting customers' identities and data, enabling better working conditions and quality of life, eradicating corruption and supporting governance of states; all of these aspects will actually build a better business climate as well. Win-Win-Win. Opportunity and risk are just different sides of the same coin.

Risks from How We Behave – Conduct Risks

To reflect on the multifaceted view of risk concerning how things are done, we use the term *conduct risk* in this book. Conduct risks include both how the company is behaving in terms of internal rules and expectations and how the company behaves towards those external to the corporation.

Managing risk is a central part of conducting business – every opportunity comes with a risk – either you ignore the risk and plough through, blinded by the opportunity ahead or you decide to get to know the situation better. Companies identify risks that may affect their business and ability to reach set targets and classify these into categories such as strategic risks, legal risks, operational risks, financial risks, security risks, political risks and reputational risks. Some companies may also have specific categories for sustainability, environmental or societal risks. The challenge with risks related to conduct, i.e. *how* the company does business, is that they can be categorised under several, if not all, of these risk categories. Violations of, for example, legislation pertaining to bribery and corruption, money laundering, anti-trust laws or laws on discrimination can be categorised as legal or compliance risks, or as financial risks due to penalties or losses, as reputational risks because of the negative media attention or sometimes as sustainability risks (maybe because it is the "sustainability folks" who seem to care most about these risks?). Financial or reputational risks commonly arise as a consequence of conduct failure, for example, violation of laws or ethical norms such as the UN Global Compact. The company may also have set standards through internal rules such as the Code of Conduct, policies or statements made by leaders or in sustainability or annual reports and a violation of these rules or statements may carry the same financial and reputational risks.

Risk management in a company is a process to identify, assess and mitigate risks from the *company's* perspective. But a responsible company goes beyond its own perspective and understands that the company, through its behaviour, exposes *others* to risks as well. This can also be described as a debt built over time owed to society, the environment and individuals. The debt is an indirect cost that is not paid by the company but by people who are working in sub-standard labour conditions (for example, so that the company can sell cheap clothes). Paid by society at large, when bribes are paid to authorities for a government license or permit. A debt is created towards the people of a country where kleptocracy distorts distribution of national wealth. While the company is reaping the benefits, this invisible debt is growing. Then something happens, an article in a newspaper or a TV programme or a tweet that spreads like fire and the debt is exposed to the public eye. The risk from the corporate conduct is materialising, at which time a crisis or a scandal will be followed by more tangible legal, reputational and financial consequences.

A calculation of risk and reward

Every recalled or repurchased VW diesel car in this lot at Old Detroit Lions Stadium represents the sum of an economic calculation made by the company between risk and reward. In that way VW is not so different from other companies. They see themselves as financial abstractions pressured by competition to build models on profit, loss and market share. But when many of us think of the lungs of our children, scarred by NOx fumes that could

have been contained, we wonder if the equation is missing an important variable?

Netflix Dirty Money

To be able to design your compliance programme, including organisation, governance and possible remedial efforts, in a sufficient way, you should start with a *Conduct Risk Assessment*. The objective with conduct risk assessment is to ensure that you understand the external realities and internal constraints that ultimately foster and guide the corporate conduct.

A Model for Conduct Risk Assessment

The framework for our conduct risk assessment is concise and we have deliberately designed it this way to ensure that it is usable and not a theoretical and overwhelming exercise. Input for your conduct risk assessment is gathered from three main sources: 1) from assessing your internal context and developing your self-knowledge, 2) from the external context; talking with and understanding the requirements of your stakeholders including the regulatory stakeholders, and non-governmental organisations, and 3) understanding the impact your business has on human rights. By developing your self-knowledge, you will understand risks from the company culture. By listening to your stakeholders and assessing relevant regulatory frameworks, you will understand

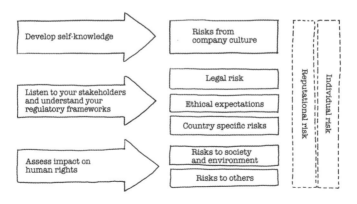

particular risks arising from working in specific countries, legal risks and ethical expectations. Furthermore, by assessing your human rights impact, you will identify risks for society and the environment and risks caused to others. Poor self-knowledge and a weak understanding of stakeholder expectations and your impact on human rights will also ultimately result in reputational risks and possibly even individual risks for the directors and decision makers.

Develop Self-Knowledge

To analyse and understand your own business and your own company sounds like a no-brainer, right? You may however be surprised by how many different opinions there are in the company on how the company actually works. Some-times, it is a challenge just 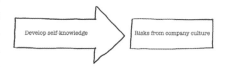 to understand the legal structures, ownership situation and gover-nance of local companies. A global company may have fully func-tioning boards in wholly or majority-owned subsidiaries, while others may work with boards in subsidiaries only for legal and administrative purposes. A support function may be called "global", but in reality is not a global function, as some business regions or local units are excluded for variety of reasons. The group policies may not be consistently implemented in subsidiaries and joint ventures, and there may be lack of global processes for approving and documenting exceptions from group policies and procedures. In developing self-knowledge, it is important to understand how decisions are really made: are they made in the designated forums or in fact in informal discussions and pre-meetings? How openly are risks of corruption in a sales deal discussed and how confident are employees about raising concerns? Are there certain topics that are never discussed, for example, sexual harassment or drunkenness by a senior executive?

We realise that corporate culture is difficult to identify, assess and describe, but this is not an excuse for lack of action. There are aspects of the corporate culture that management may have an interest in building and supporting, such as customer orientation, high performance, innovation and creativity. But these efforts can be undermined by a lack of understanding of aspects relating to corporate conduct such as allowing differing opinions, ensuring diversity and inclusivity and creating space for speaking up and openness. Retaliation, harassment, fear and oppression as well as pushing too hard for financial results and sales with limited regard for risk will be detrimental for all cultural aspirations.

When exploring the internal context in order to build self-awareness we have found entire business units surrounded by rumours of indefinable threats and security problems, allowing for exceptions from corporate rules and practices. We have met managers who are considered "heroes", who have delivered unmatchable growth during the past years while working in "hostile" environments and therefore must not be "disturbed" by group directives or "policing" functions such as Internal Audit or Ethics & Compliance. Heroes that get away with "small" exceptions to the rules and corporate values, maybe excessive or inappropriate business entertainment or lax controls of travel expenses, discriminatory language or all-white-male management team, to more concerning exceptions such as opaque charity contributions, use of unjustifiable local business partners, advisors or obscure local subcontractors. Such exceptions create an excellent environment for fraud, corruption, bribery and cronyism. Strong regional head offices far away from the group, where they mock people at HQ who cannot seem to understand that things "are done differently here", are also warning signals for an unhealthy corporate sub-culture, which you may want to look further into when building your framework for managing corporate conduct.

One dimension of assessing the "self" is to understand risks originating from the history, the *legacy risks*. The compliance requirements, when it comes to certain conduct risks, for example, corruption and harassment, are more strict today than they were ten or even five years ago. The result may be that you have historic business transactions and agreements that are still valid but would not hold up to public or regulatory scrutiny today.

There may also be internal policies and processes that need to be revisited with new eyes. Maybe, the company's view on business entertainment has (or should be) changed since the last revision of the policy? Maybe, there are old processes and registers that cannot support new requirements for protection of the integrity and privacy of your customers? We have found that most people are very supportive when it comes to improving processes and behaviour going forwards but are sometimes more sceptical when it comes to looking backwards. The best sales pitch from our side has been that it is better for us as a company to be aware of the skeletons and deal with them, instead of leaving them for others to find. As we see in corporate scandals, the misconduct often happened five or ten years ago, so it is better to clean up your act and legacy issues before someone else decides to.

Probably one of the most important blog posts in 2017

On 19 February 2017, Susan Fowler, a former engineer at Uber Technologies, Inc. published a blog post detailing allegations of harassment, discrimination, retaliation and ineffectiveness of the company's policies and procedures. The post received massive attention and spread like wildfire, resulting in articles in prominent newspapers and other media, forcing the Board of Uber to spring into action, by appointing a law firm to conduct a thorough and objective review of "the specific issues related to the workplace environment raised by Susan Fowler as well as diversity and inclusion at Uber more broadly". The board also appointed a "Special Committee" to oversee the

review. The law firm took the assignment seriously, partnered up with relevant experts, conducted more than 200 interviews and reviewed available documents and emails. After hearing the law firm's conclusions, the Board of Directors at Uber unanimously adopted all the recommendations made by the law firm. The recommendations for remedial actions listed were substantial and included changes to senior leadership, including changes in responsibilities of the CEO, increased profile and empowerment of the Head of Diversity, measurements and metrics for senior leadership on the cultural aspects at hand. The Board of Directors at Uber were further recommended to: 1) incorporate ethical business practices, diversity and inclusion as well as other values from Uber's Code of Conduct in its extensive compensation programme; 2) nominate a senior executive to oversee the implementation of the recommendations; 3) improve controls, enhance board oversight, and conduct mandatory leadership and human resources training on matters such as retaliation, harassment, inclusion and handling of employee complaints; 4) improve and enhance complaints and escalation processes; 5) establish an employee diversity advisory board, publish diversity statistics, target diverse sources of talent and conduct blind resume reviews; 6) substantially improve policies and practices, as well as implementation thereof; 7) modify performance reviews to avoid bias and misuse, set clear goals, follow-up on these and measure performance against the goals; and 8) conduct exit-interviews.

In short, implement an ethics and compliance programme.

On 21 June 2017, Travis Kalanick, co-founder and CEO of Uber, resigned from his role as CEO, after being requested to do so by a group of large investors. Not so surprisingly, in August of the same year, the US authorities opened an inquiry related to payments abroad, targeting possible violations of laws related to bribery overseas.

Research indicates that if culture becomes corrupt[11] and a separation between words and action institutionalises misconduct[12], the problem will not only be issues such as corrupt payments but will also create an environment that is vulnerable to fraud and embezzlement. An internal context dominated by saying one thing and doing another can also

11 Jamie-Lee Campbell and Anja S. Göritz. Culture Corrupts! A Qualitative Study of Organizational Culture in Corrupt Organizations. Journal of Business Ethics (2014), 120: 291–311.

12 Tammy L. MacLean and Michael Benham. The Dangers of Decoupling: The Relationship Between Compliance Programs, Legitimacy Perceptions and Institutionalized Misconduct. Academy of Management Journal. (2010), 53 (6): 1499–1520.

become expensive and according to an estimate by the Association of Certified Fraud Examiners corporate fraud eats up 5 % of the annual revenues[13]. If you allow a culture to build unchecked, you may end up with one that harms your business, your employees and your brand. A bad culture requires intensive care and extraordinary measures to reverse. A culture of harassment, discrimination, poor inclusion and sloppy attitudes towards policies and processes will inevitably also lead to additional harmful misbehaviour, such as fraud, bribery and conflict of interest. By putting words into action, by doing what you are saying, systematically and consistently, this negative culture can be reversed and an ethical culture will start to emerge.

Assessing the Internal Context – a checklist

- ✓ Ownership structure, local partners and joint ventures?
- ✓ Legal structure, responsibility and authority of subsidiary boards?
- ✓ Organisational structure: what is the responsibility and authority of a central function in a matrix organisation?
- ✓ Governance: how are group policies implemented in subsidiaries and small sales offices?
- ✓ Controls: who is designing and, more importantly, who is implementing the internal controls, how is effectiveness monitored and issues corrected?
- ✓ Competence: is there sufficient and qualified ethics and compliance expertise, not only at the corporate level but also in the business functions?
- ✓ Third parties, dependency on outsourced services, certain suppliers and sales model, are own employees doing the sales activities or are we relying on intermediaries?
- ✓ Legacy issues, risks from historic agreements and unresolved whistle-blowing reports?
- ✓ Assess the culture (see questions below).

---

13 https://s3-us-west-2.amazonaws.com/acfepublic/2018-report-to-the-nations.pdf

The perfect storm – Black clouds of corporate culture

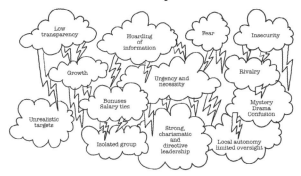

Assess the Culture – some questions

- ✓ Is growth the primary strategic target?

- ✓ Are there unrealistic sales goals, especially without consideration of drastic changes in market conditions?

- ✓ Are the bonus targets tied to sales (no regard for profitability or risk)?

- ✓ Is there a strong sense of urgency and ad hoc mentality?

- ✓ Is there a tendency towards not sharing information, using information as power and of leaders "hoarding" information?

- ✓ Is there a fear of talking about challenges and risks?

- ✓ Is there a sense of fear, rivalry, insecurity and powerlessness?

- ✓ Do we accept that strong leaders or important groups should not be questioned or scrutinised?

- ✓ Do we have isolated parts of the organisation where common processes and systems or additional controls are not implemented – either by circumstance or design?

- ✓ Is there an acceptance of local autonomy with limited oversight, existence of sub-cultures and corporate heroes?

- ✓ Are corporate heroes allowed to play by their own rules because they always exceed the sales targets?

- ✓ Are formal decisions changed or diluted by informal actions and superficial implementation?

Listen to Your Stakeholders and Understand Your Regulatory Framework

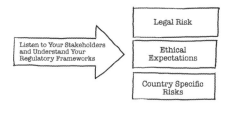

Who are the corporation's stakeholders? The answer "the shareholders" is not the entire and simple truth anymore. Is the company creating a debt towards the environment, society and humans or are they balancing their use of resources in a responsible way? To fully manage the corporate conduct, the important stakeholders must be identified. Boards have a fiduciary duty towards the shareholders, who have put them there to protect their interests, but does that preclude them from also considering other interests? Do the laws on corporate governance and fiduciary duties prevent boards and companies from looking further than shareholders' interests to build value? Eccles and Youmans[14] argue that boards not only can but should consider stakeholders' interests in a wider sense when determining material issues for strategy and reporting; they further argue that most laws on corporate governance allow for such considerations.

Well prepared and executed stakeholder dialogue is a helpful tool in understanding your external context and expectations. Whom to invite to the stakeholder dialogue is dependent on your business and operations; you may find the country risk assessments shedding some light on stakeholders that you might not think of normally. Make sure to invite people from organisations that can represent the voiceless stakeholders, such as Human Rights Watch, representing people who live in a corrupt and kleptocratic society or in a country where labour rights are disregarded. Your whole industry may also

---

14   Eccles, R. G. and Youmans, T. (2016), Materiality in Corporate Governance: The Statement of Significant Audiences and Materiality. Journal of Applied Corporate Finance, 28: 39–46.

have specific commonalities when it comes to voiceless stakeholders, such as problematic conflict minerals in the electronic industries. We have discussed the possibility of inviting a journalist to the stakeholder dialogue: there are pros and cons such as confidentiality concerns. However, for some companies, it may not be a bad idea. Other examples include important customers and suppliers, relevant partners, labour organisations/unions, relevant non-profit organisations, such as UNICEF who can represent children's rights, to mention only a few potential invitees. Organising the dialogue as a series of reasonably-sized roundtable discussions is both a useful and enjoyable exercise. We have found it to be a good idea to use an external professional to moderate the roundtables; it creates an atmosphere of neutrality and professionalism and ensures that there is a diligent person to take minutes and help with the analysis.

We have also experimented with sending out stakeholder surveys, which we found to be less useful than roundtable discussions but certainly also less time consuming. A survey can be a complement to roundtable discussions, to reach a larger group, focus the discussion on certain topics or to understand whom to invite to the roundtables.

A stakeholder approach

Atlas Copco is registered in Sweden and is legally governed by the Swedish Companies Act (2005:551). This act requires that the Board of Directors govern the company to be profitable and create value for its shareholders. However, Atlas Copco recognise going beyond this, that by integrating sustainability into its business it creates long-term value for all stakeholders, which is ultimately in the best interest of the company, the shareholders and society. The significant sta-

keholder audience, as outlined in the Atlas Copco Business Code of Practice, includes representatives of society, employees, customers, business partners and shareholders. The Business Code of Practice is the central guiding policy for Atlas Copco and is owned by the Board of Directors. Its commitment goes beyond the requirements of legal compliance, to support voluntary international ethical guidelines. These include the United Nations International Bill of Human Rights, International Labour Organisation Declaration on Fundamental Principles and Rights at Work, the ten principles of the United Nations Global Compact, and OECDs Guidelines for Multinational Enterprises. Atlas Copco has used a stakeholder-driven approach in order to identify the most material environmental, human rights, labour and ethical aspects for its business. These priorities guide how the Group develops and drives its business strategy, as well as its roadmap to support the UN Sustainable Development Goals.

http://www.atlascopcogroup.com/en/sustainability/our-sustainability-approach/our-business-code-of-practice

Legal Risk

In assessing what legal and regulatory frameworks are relevant, it is important to keep a broad view on jurisdictional reach. Many countries have introduced legislation on bribery and corruption that reaches far beyond the traditional view on jurisdictional reach: extraterritorial reach. The US FCPA, the UK Bribery Act and the new French Sapin II Loi are examples of this. It may seem wrong, opportunistic and a way to strengthen the state finances when companies, so far away from the origin of both its home country as well as the location where the crime is committed, are forced to pay mindboggling fines and disgorgements. When the UK Bribery Act was introduced, we participated in several workshops where British law firms repeatedly brought up how outrageous the Act was in its outreach – well, it is here and we might as well get used to the fact that more countries will join the force of globalisation and adopt laws that reach far outside their borders. Even as recently as 2012, when Telia Company asked a law firm to do an independent investigation on whether or not the conduct related to market entry in Uzbekistan was legal or not, the company limited the relevant legal frameworks to Swedish and Uzbek law. Two years later, in spring 2014, both the US and Dutch prosecutor opened investigations against the company on corruption, which finally lead to a 965 MUSD deferred prosecution agreement in September 2017.

It is not only conduct risks of bribery and corruption that are regulated through extraterritorial legislation. There is, for example, the EU privacy regulations, EU and US anti-trust regulations, a new UK legislation on slavery and forced labour (in the supply chain); moreover, the trend is for increased extraterritorial legislation and complexity. On the bright side, some legislations give credit to companies that have implemented effective compliance programmes. In the US, it is not only the FCPA (Foreign Corrupt Practices Act) that identifies, describes and gives credit to an effective compliance programme (evidenced in, for example, the Telia Company case), it is also applicable for occupational health and safety matters in OSHA. The new French corruption legislation (Sapin II Loi) require all companies operating in France with more than 500 employees to implement an anti-bribery corruption compliance programme. The UK Bribery Act credits adequate compliance programmes; in Spain, the criminal code was reformed in 2010 to include corporate criminal liability, and Spain has subsequently introduced requirements of crime prevention, in effect compliance programmes.

Why should US act as the world police?

When speaking about ethics and compliance, and more specifically anti-bribery compliance, I'm often asked the question of why the US FCPA law is applicable for a Swedish, Finnish or Dutch company. When I explain the extraterritorial nature of the law, the response often is why should the US be the world's policeman? A relevant question, considering for example the questionable lobbying system in Washington DC. One can argue about the right of the US to take a lead on global corruption enforcement, but the fact is that without the US law, resources and experience in the field, we would not have seen as many clean ups as we have. Without the FCPA, enacted already in the 1970s, it is unlikely that the world would have turned their attention to the actual harm and suffering created by global corruption. It may seem unfair, of course, that a Swedish company has to pay fines and disgorgement in the tune of 965 MUSD to the US and the Netherlands; you might think that it would be much better if the money was paid to the Swedish Government instead. Well, I agree and this is probably exactly what the French realised after the big Alstom case, where the French power and transportation company agreed to pay a record of 772 MUSD to the US Government in 2015, for bribery to government officials in Indonesia, Saudi Arabia, Egypt, the Bahamas and Taiwan. One does not have to be very conspiratorial to assume that this fact, along with a sense of ethical and legal failure, weighed in when the French managed to get the new corruption law, Sapin II Loi enacted in record time. It is a law on corruption that takes after the US FCPA, when it comes to corporate liability, global settlements, new levels of fines and disgorgement and includes regulated requirements for anti-bribery compliance programmes. I hope Sweden and many more countries will follow, ensuring that its legislation is suitable for tackling global corruption – then the US would not have to play such a big role anymore. It will, however, take some time before other authorities build up the capacity and skills to investigate these complex cases. So, US support is likely to be needed for some time still…and regardless of who does the job, the most important thing will still be to promote fair business and fair competition.

Ethical Expectations

Whether a company has signed up to the UN Global Compact or not, these guidelines create a global baseline for expectations on corporate behaviour. There are other organisations and guidelines, such as ILO (International Labour Organisation, a tri-party organisation bringing governments, employers and workers perspectives together to support and develop rights at work) or OECD with Guidelines for Multinational Enterprises. When it comes to corporate behaviour, it is not enough to turn to the legal department for an opinion on what is legal or illegal; this is relevant information for a lot of purposes, but not for understanding how much trouble the company may find itself in from neglecting to assess and understand the global framework of norms and ethical expectations.

Understanding ethics and current norms also enables you to understand the relevant legal framework for conduct risks much better. It enables board members and other executives, with limited time on their hands, to ask relevant questions on legal opinions.

We have to assume that regulations and legislations are based on common norms and values, and, with few exceptions, the legislative process is slow. In trying to ensure that what you do and decide today is perceived as the right thing to do in some years' time, you are supported by a good understanding of common norms and values. This is not altogether an easy task as common norms and values change over time and if you are not assessing your context periodically with the right competences and human intelligence applied, you might miss these changes. Just look at tax planning and the common view on what companies can and cannot do. Starbucks missed the change in perception on what is the right thing to do and ended up in a costly scandal in the UK.

A changed world – Starbucks in trouble

In 2012, Starbucks ended up with a big customer backlash, and the UK executives were called before a Parliamentary Committee hearing as news agency Reuters reported that Starbucks had paid just 8,6 MGBP in corporation tax in the UK over 14 years and nothing at all during the past three years due to the way it had arranged its business affairs. Despite there being no illegality, Starbucks was seen as not doing the right thing and was punished by their customers. Eventually, in a move that was described by tax lawyers as "unprecedented", Starbucks agreed to voluntarily pay "a significant amount of tax, irrelevant if the company was legally obligated to or not. "We are going to do what is required beyond the law".

What was fine, even commendable some years ago, is not okay at all anymore and even if setting up holding companies on small islands with warm climates for tax purposes might be legal, it is not in tune with common values and ethical expectations anymore.

Country Specific Risk

A fundamental aspect of conduct risk will originate from the country where the company operates. There is a pitfall in believing that being a company with strong values will automatically mitigate the risks of operating in a high-risk jurisdiction, for example, in a country with oppressive regimes and with different views on human rights. How are the institutions such as the political system, legal system, the courts, the educational system, and the financial system run? How is power distributed and passed on? Are there clans or families who control the country? Is there a kleptocractic inheritance? If so, is this in combination with a strong security force at the disposal of the government? Are there basic human rights such as freedom of speech and access to justice or not? Is there a mix-up or connection between public and private sector? How is the church or religious community related to power, business life, fortune and governance in the country? What is the present situation and the outlook for the country including its history?

In your dialogue with stakeholders, you will get input on country specific traits. There is a lot of information to be found on the Internet as well; we have found the World Bank Doing Business and Business Against Corruption portals to be useful.[15] For countries that are not so complex, which have solid governments and institutions, a thorough and professional desktop search might provide ample information for a good report on country risk. However, if the country is more complex and obscure, you may need help from professionals or scholars with a specific knowledge of the country and region. Companies tend to work in silos, so do not be surprised if you find that a lot of information is already in the company but not added up, analysed, compiled and put together in a report, available for all who may need this very useful information. As the reports must also be available to executive

15 http://www.doingbusiness.org/; http://www.business-anti-corruption.com/

management, including the board of directors, you may need an executive summary for each country.

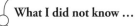

The first time I requested a thorough country risk assessment was for Iran many years ago – despite having travelled to the country several times and meeting business people both internally and externally, the report, which was well written and a pleasure to read, opened my eyes. I had seen myself as a seasoned business traveller in the region, but it turned out that I knew almost nothing about how the country was actually run and governed, the concept of "deep state" and what role it had in state finance, government control, banking and private business, which families and groups were important or not and how the people were controlled. When Anna and I started working together in Telia Company, compiling country risk assessments for all the countries in the business area Eurasia was one of the first things we did. The reports put meat on the bones, and instead of speaking of "challenging countries" or "corruption" in broad terms, the new management and we had access to much more specific knowledge. To start with, the knowledge that not all countries in our business area Eurasia

were the same – it's interesting how easy it is to make that mistake. Just look at some US based companies that think that all of Europe is the same just because they have put all their European operations in one business unit called "Europe". Or why not some European companies that think all of Africa is the same and have business area "MEA – Middle East Africa", headquartered in Dubai, visited mostly for the convenient airport and excellent hotels. From the country reports in Telia Company, we gained more structured knowledge about countries with absolute power and lack of democratic processes, random death penalty use, forced labour, kleptocracy enabling the ultimate power to access great wealth normally belonging to the state and its people, cronyism, nepotism, secret police to keep people in place, lack of freedom of speech, dysfunctional financial systems, currency restrictions, lack of independent courts, poverty, illiteracy and broken infrastructure. This was important information, not only to us in the E&C team and for building an effective Anti-Bribery Corruption programme but also for all functions in the company working with the business region.

A Human Rights Impact Assessment (HRIA) simplifies the complexity of managing human rights by providing companies with a consistent, efficient and systematic way to identify, prioritise and address human rights risks and opportunities at a corporate, country, site or product level.

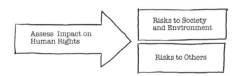

A HRIA is a valuable tool to gain corporate experience on how the company and its business are perceived from another angle. It engages many people, both inside and outside of your company and also increases the awareness internally that human rights is not separate from business and that rights such as freedom from corruption, privacy, health and safety, and labour practices are matched by collective (companies, states, NGOs, etc.) and individual (each of us) responsibilities. A HRIA will also make visible that conduct risks often are violations of human rights. Simply put, HRIA is an exercise of assessing what human rights the company might be impacting. You turn the lens away from your own interests and risks and take a good look at who the business of the company affects and how. A HRIA involves interviewing people outside of the company such as experts in human rights, NGOs, representatives from government, suppliers, important customers, and inside the company such as factory workers, accountants and senior managers. To ensure a pragmatic approach, it may be best to conduct a HRIA on country level and involve the leadership in that specific country as well as group level leadership. We have found the tools available from BSR[16] and the Danish Institute for Human Rights to be helpful.[17]

16 https://www.bsr.org/

17 https://www.humanrights.dk/business/tools/human-rights-impact-assessment-guidance-and-toolbox

Bribery and corruption are nothing new, but the world's view and acceptance of corruption has changed dramatically over the past years. As the old UN Millennium goals were reworked into the new SDG, Transparency International (TI) in 2013 published  recommendations to the UN,[18] pointing out that the major obstacle for achieving the goals was, and continues to be, global systemic corruption and weak government governance – an aspect that had been left out from the initial UN Millennium goals. In the new SDG, TIs concerns are reflected in SDG 16 (Promote peaceful and inclusive societies for sustainable development, provide access to justice for all, and build effective, accountable and inclusive institutions on all levels). Companies can make an active decision as to whether they are part of the problem, submitting to weak local government governance or part of the solution, working systematically, understanding and improving the external context. Companies may, through their operations, be complicit in feeding weak local structures, structures where formal processes are circumvented by bribes, structures where labour rights can be violated by "purchasing a formal certificate", structures where nepotism is at the core of the society, or structures where bribes have to be paid to access public healthcare services. Not to forget the banks who enable the kleptocrts moving bribes in to "the system". Understanding how human rights, the rights of individuals in the societies where the company is present, are impacted by the business's operations is important, and more and more companies are embracing this aspect of understanding and assessing risks that

---

18   https://www.transparency.org/news/feature/building_anti_corruption_into_the_millennium_
     development_goals

the company exposes others to. While this is a great development and puts global corporations in a position to provide meaningful change for people who suffer from human rights abuses, it is also an area where we have found that companies talk more than they walk. For that reason alone, it is a good idea to put this risk category in the overall risk process of the company and in the model for conduct risks. To fully comprehend and assess Societal/Human Rights risks, you need to have a very good view on the company's supply chain as well as third parties. This is a daunting task for many, and it certainly has been for us. We come back to this topic again and again, fix the supply chain and know your third parties – it may not be done tomorrow, but it must be done.

Reputational Risk

It is not uncommon that conduct risks are bundled up and classified as reputational risk. This is not at all surprising as we watch conduct risks turn from risk to crisis and reputational damage all the time. In the end, it does not matter much if the misconduct was illegal or unethical or not, the damage has been done through relentless media coverage and reputational damage. We are not communications experts and this book is not about how to build and maintain a great brand but it is sufficient to repeat the wise words of whoever said them first; to build a brand takes many years, to destroy it takes a few minutes.

Reputation is always a consequence of what is done or of what is left undone, not a core risk in itself.

However, we prefer not to categorise conduct risks in reputational risk. We suggest that reputational risk and damages are rather consequential risks, hence, consequence of bad behaviour, misjudgements and opportunistic decisions. This is important only for one, significant, reason – if you don't understand that the conduct risk is really, at its core, an ethical/legal or societal risk but assume it is a reputational risk, you may conclude that the media are writing the risk agenda for the company, supporting a feeling of victimisation and defensiveness. Conduct risk management will become all about communication and not really undertaking work to tackle the actual problem and root cause for the media upheaval, the conduct failure.

Individual Risk

In addressing corporate conduct risks and their impact, it is appropriate to also mention individual risk. Behaviour is always attributable to a person, as a legal entity is not capable of "behaving". This means that in making decisions and taking action on behalf of the company, you may put yourself at risk. Board members and executive management have insurances for most financial consequences, but such insurances do not cover having to go to jail for paying or approving bribes or losing your position or good reputation. For employees who are not insured, they stand to lose a great deal by acting on behalf of the company. Regulators have increasingly identified that companies tend to "pay and move on" without remorse or improvement; therefore, there is an increasing trend to prosecute individuals, in addition to the company.[19] There is also an expectation from regulators that the company has taken appropriate disciplinary action against individuals involved or enabling the misconduct. To say that you have stopped the payments but not disciplined the person who approved the payments will not be well perceived at the DOJ in Washington or

---

19   On 9 September 2015, Deputy Attorney General, Sally Q. Yates issued a memorandum entitled, "Individual Accountability for Corporate Wrongdoing", the memo states that "one of the most effective ways to combat corporate misconduct is by seeking accountability from the individuals who perpetrated the wrongdoing". https://www.justice.gov/archives/dag/file/769036/download

SFO in London. By being complicit in corrupt activity, by turning a blind eye or by not speaking up, managers and decision makers put themselves at risk. This is an important aspect of any compliance related training. The compliance program may protect the company, but not the individual who decides to violate the rules or is negligent.

Your Company - Your Content

Once you understand the context and identify and assess the conduct risks, you will know where to start and what to prioritise in your work with corporate conduct. Many companies choose to prioritise the anti-bribery corruption programme (ABC programme). It's for a good reason; if you do the ABC programme properly it will provide a foundation for covering other ethics and compliance topics. This is the reason you will find that we often refer to the ABC programme implementation, but we want to underline that all corporate conduct compliance programmes, such as respecting the privacy of individuals, harassment, diversity and inclusion, ensuring a safe working environment, competing fairly, and complying with sanctions and export control rules as well as preventing money laundering can be structured, based on the same principles and framework.

A challenge in establishing the content is typically priority and focus. It is normal with boards and bosses to want to do everything at the same time, but most of the time it is not possible; so to avoid a large gap between talk and walk (words and action), prioritising and focusing are essential. There will always be a certain gap between talk and action; for example, a leader can say that he or she "has zero tolerance of corruption", but for the organisation to achieve "zero tolerance", there is a long way to go; in fact, it might be unachievable but the organisation keeps on trying and stays forward leaning. This might be productive and force support for the actions required, somewhat similar to making a personal statement of running the New York marathon to force yourself to train. However, if you are in bad shape to start with and don't really have time to practise enough, the New York Marathon will most probably be incredibly painful and a failure. So, stay focused and transparent regarding what you want to achieve and what actually is achievable with the current resources and priorities.

Commonly, the overall principles relating to the aspired corporate conduct are specified in a Code of Conduct. We will describe in more detail how to structure a Code of Conduct in the following chapter on building your ethics and compliance programme.

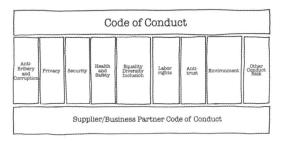

Do Not Forget Those Representing You

The responsibility for corporate conduct includes the whole value and supply chain. Some may disagree and try to contractually regulate and disown responsibility. However, many corporate scandals originate from risks in the supply chain or from sales intermediaries. In the BP Deepwater Horizon catastrophe it was not BP that operated the platform but Transocean, a contractor to large oil companies companies in the world. Nevertheless, BP was the one who bore the consequences of legal, financial and reputational risks, not to forget the consequences to the surrounding environment, the local villagers, the ocean and wildlife. It was not Nestlé that had forced labor on their payroll but one of their contractors in the fishing industry in Thailand. This led to terrible media coverage and lost customer trust (reputational and financial risks) but ultimately at the core was the fishermen's poor working conditions and pitiful salary, risks borne by the fisherman. And Rolls Royce got into trouble for what their sales intermediaries, dealers, agents and consultants were hired to do.

Your agents, resellers, vendors and business partners might not even know what is expected from them, when it comes to how they are expected to act even if they have signed a Supplier or Business Partner Code of Conduct. But as you will see in the chapter on Third Party Management, the same rigour should be applied for third party management as for internal work.

Swedish Government Scrambles to Contain Damage From Data Breach

By CHRISTINA ANDERSON 25 JULY 2017

The New York Times

STOCKHOLM — Sweden's government is scrambling to contain the political fallout from a huge breach of confidential data, including the possible disclosure of the identities of undercover operatives, under the watch of a government contractor.

The breach was disclosed this month by the Swedish newspaper Dagens Nyheter, when it reported that Maria Agren, the former Director General of the Swedish Transport Agency, had been fired in January for negligent handling of classified data.

The agency entered into an outsourcing agreement with IBM Sweden in April 2015, worth nearly $100 million, to manage vehicle registration and driver's license databases. But adequate safeguards were not adopted, and as a result, unauthorized personnel at IBM subsidiaries in Eastern Europe had access to vast troves of sensitive information, including details about bridges, roads, ports, the subway system in Stockholm and other infrastructure.

In addition, the identities of people working undercover for the Swedish police and the Swedish security service, known as Sapo, may have been revealed, along with names of people working undercover for the special intelligence unit of the Swedish armed forces.

https://www.nytimes.com/2017/07/25/world/europe/ibm-sweden-data-outsourcing.html

Chapter FIVE

Compliance – from Words to Action

In the previous chapters, we have discussed why improvements to corporate conduct are needed, why we should care about more than just the immediate financial returns and current share price. We have discussed how to understand what to actually work with and how to prioritise to secure long-term financial returns and retain stakeholder value. Corporate resources, time, money and people are scarce, and it is important that the work is based on what really matters for the company and its stakeholders, and that the work focuses on what the company can and should impact. To understand the context and define the content is like setting the scene. It is defining how the company cares about the environment and clean business, about being a responsible corporate citizen and putting ambitions into words. The next step is to put the words into action, to ensure that the company actually is walking the talk, and builds credibility and trust because what is said is also actually being done. The framework for corporate conduct is a tool for implementation and practical application. A tool that can and should be applied to any area of expected conduct described in the code of ethics and conduct. It will provide both internal stakeholders such as boards and executive management teams as well as external stakeholders such as analysts, investors and social interest groups a framework for how to assess what is actually done. Is there any action beyond the words?

We argue that many corporate scandals originate from there being too many words but no corresponding action to ensure compliance with those words. What the media is doing is simply visualising this gap by showing the public that the words are only that, words without true meaning. For us, the words are important but public commitment and CEO statements are just the beginning – so let's get to work.

Our framework for managing corporate conduct describes effective compliance or adequate procedures, as a company would be required to demonstrate if tested on the subject by a regulator or authority, for example, the DOJ in the US or SFO in the UK.[20] How you choose to illustrate your compliance model is a matter of taste, as long as all the elements are there. We have had the opportunity to use our framework in making presentations to boards and managements, investors, journalists, fellow ethics, compliance and sustainability workers and to the authorities in several important jurisdictions. The framework has enabled systematic reporting and follow-up of the work, in the respective areas of corporate conduct. Our conclusion is to stick to the programme and improve it year after year – never leaving one aspect of the full model aside.

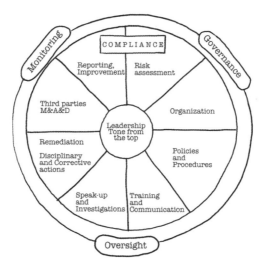

---

20 https://www.ussc.gov/guidelines/2015-guidelines-manual/2015-chapter-8; http://www.justice.gov.uk/downloads/legislation/bribery-act-2010-guidance.pdf

The compliance model describes eight cornerstones of compliance: [1] risk assessment, [2] organisation, [3] policies and procedures, [4] training and communication, [5] speaking up and investigations, [6] remediation, disciplinary and corrective actions, [7] third parties and [8] reporting and improvement. The model is founded on strong leadership (tone from the top), and supported by governance, monitoring and oversight at the management and board level. Working diligently with compliance also challenges and strengthens the core of the programme, leadership. In the following chapter, we will provide some insights into what each of the cornerstones of the compliance model entails.

> **Working diligently with compliance also challenges and strengthens the core of the programme – leadership.**

Risk Assessment

The work with understanding the context and content is where you understand the big picture, the risk exposure from the outside and from the inside. But for each area of expected conduct, you will have to dig deeper into the operations to understand the day-to-day operational risks. The fundamental requirement of any ethics and compliance programme is that it is risk-based and tailored to the company's specific traits.

Management teams may have bad experiences from receiving complex and long risk reports, where you can't see the forest for the trees. Not to mention board members who may find the risk reporting from the management overwhelming or way too simplistic with a "best guess risk heat map" (probability/impact). Having an Enterprise Risk Management (ERM) process is increasingly common, and while an ERM process may be both required and beneficial, it can result in an information overload on the *what* aspect of the business and lack of information on the *how* aspect of doing business. In addition, the pitfall of risk reports is that the risks are reported from one year to another with limited follow-up and understanding of what is actually being done to mitigate and manage these risks. We have deliberately avoided addressing the methodology of risk management, as there is plenty of literature on that. For reference, see COSO newly updated guidance on ERM.[21] We will also not be talking in great detail about risk appetite, risk tolerance, risk mitigation and residual risk. These are, however, important concepts to understand but not as theoretical concepts but in practice. You will have to consider and agree about how much risk you want to accept and how much risk you can live with. However, assessing conduct risk should not be done in isolation; it is in the nature of compliance workers to focus on the risk relating to, for example, the use of a particular sales agent, while sales people focus on winning the deal and the revenue and the risk of not reaching targets. Alignment is needed, relating to how much risk will be left when you have done everything you can [or want to] do, to handle the risk. In some cases, the risk someone in the company has decided to accept is something that the ethics and compliance officer will have to transparently escalate and visualise to the appropriate level of management, ultimately to executive management and the board. An ethics and compliance officer and a sales manager may not always agree with what is an acceptable level of risk. The important thing is to uphold transparency and ensure that the risk is not silently accepted or hidden in the organisation.

Risk assessment is a recurring, very hands-on exercise, not a paper product. It is in practice very simple, and a lot of the pre-work and analysis can be done as desktop work. Nonetheless, do not underestimate the importance and value of going onsite,

21 https://www.coso.org/Pages/erm.aspx

visiting remote locations, understanding how the business there actually operates and what their daily reality is like. In some of the companies that we have worked with, we developed tools for local management to fill out questionnaires for their local operations, which saved both time and cost from actually having to travel there ourselves. It is, however, important to keep in mind that self-assessments are made by people without subject matter expertise and that the quality of the answers and consequently the conclusions may suffer from bias and lack of knowledge. In some companies, we travelled to each subsidiary in high-risk countries, sat down with local management and other key functions, and spent a week going through the questions and getting a better common understanding of the risks.

It was time well spent as without these risk assessment workshops we would not have been able to set up a relevant priority for the compliance programme. They built not only our own competence and understanding but also the local management's understanding of what the risks are, how they should be taken into account and – not least – how any gaps or unacceptable exposure/practices should be remediated. We recognise that corporate resources are limited and that there will rarely be a fat budget for conducting risk assessments, but it is a necessary step in effective compliance. Specifically, it provides invaluable information for dimensioning and staffing your programme, raises the level of awareness of risk at all levels, and makes the risk visible and actionable. By reporting actual risks and scenarios to the board and management, they will get a better understanding of how to get involved and will be educated to challenge and support the programme, which is also a great demonstration of *tone from the top*.

When I worked in Middle East Africa as Head of Legal and Compliance, I wanted to travel to one of the most important markets in the entire region, Nigeria. The internal red tape for me to do the trip was overwhelming: my journey was unnecessary, it was a long flight, it was not a priority, it was this and that and finally, when I persisted, it was too dangerous. Very few people from the regional head office went because of security threats. I do not want to underplay that some cities, countries or situations do present security concerns that must be taken seriously, but I have also found that this is the perfect excuse to keep people away. I went to Lagos and I found fraud, discrimination, bribery and a terrible management style.

All risk assessment activities must be documented, what is not documented has not been done. Some parts of the risk assessment are possibly relevant and interesting for the company to make transparent externally. All parts of the risk assessment should be made available for the people working with the different compliance programmes and there should be executive summary reports going to the board and management. Sometimes, you may find yourself setting up a compliance programme for a specific area of conduct, for example, anti-bribery and corruption without having gone through an initial assessment of the internal and external context. Maybe the company is in a crisis as the media has been reporting on extravagant dinners, business trips with family members and executives appointing their friends and relatives to key positions. In this scenario, the only assessment that has been done of the context has been to read the newspapers. The company's risk process has not been mature enough to capture these conduct risks, but successively the compliance programme will build this competence. Through training, communication and follow-up, the organisation will mature to identify risks arising from how the company is behaving. If a holistic assessment of context and content has not been performed and various compliance programmes are initiated more randomly (maybe from reading newspapers or listening to lawyers and other worried consultants), there is a risk that the different compliance programmes may run parallel and repeat some aspects of the programme, re-inventing the wheel repeatedly. Coordination and cooperation are crucial.

But what if you are in a crisis, and have to get started right away, with very little time for thorough risk assessments? The immediate priority for us would be to assess and evaluate the matter at hand, dig into the root causes and assess how deep and wide the roots are. The problem may be bigger and wider spread than first anticipated. You may be required to engage investigative resources to get a more independent view of the problem and to get your arms around how it can be remediated.

When you are thrown into a crisis with the priority of fixing the problem, regaining trust and formalising the work with ethics and compliance, you also have to consider that there may be strong forces inside the company at different levels all up to management level that will do everything within their power to minimise the problem. They may be in denial mode, or afraid, or even part of the problem but, regardless of the reason, they may hide important facts and information, disrupt the investigation and prioritise self-interest before the company's best interests. This may, and is likely to, result in some friction and struggles, which are indications that some critical risks have indeed been pinpointed.

Human intelligence

Any businessperson knows that a certain risk that has been identified in a subsidiary and locally identified as a low risk (low probability and low impact) may be classified and evaluated very differently at group level (high probability and high impact). An example: in Country N it is well known that you pay a little something to the custom's officer to get your goods into the country. This is an illegal offence locally, but no one really cares because this is how it works in Country N; legal risk is viewed as low probability and low impact.

In the group office, this risk may be classified as a reputational risk with high probability and high impact, as the topic is a "hot topic" in the country where the group company is based. At group level, the company may also identify this as a legal risk with high impact, as the group office also considers and assesses extraterritorial corruption legislation outside of country N. The topic goes up on the risk heat map and risk tolerance goes down.

As the example above demonstrates, it is necessary to apply human intelligence in the risk process; otherwise, these different considerations may be lost. Automated risk processes may be efficient and cost effective; however, there is a risk that the important details are lost in the process. Human intelligence comes in the form of employees with relevant skills and experience to evaluate the situation and ensure that reasonable and relevant considerations are made. Artificial knowledge cannot replace human instinct, experience and intelligence. At least not yet.

Risk Assessment – a quick checklist

- ✓ A well-conducted Conduct Risk Assessment, which includes self-knowledge, understanding of the corporate culture, the external context, the regulatory relevant framework, stakeholder expectations and impact on human rights, society and environment will form an excellent basis for further assessing the specific conduct risks in the operations.

- ✓ Does the ERM process include conduct risks, the how business is done?

- ✓ Site visits may be necessary in countries where the risk is high or where visibility into the operations is limited.

- ✓ A risk assessment, risks identified, risks mitigated and risks absorbed or accepted should be documented in some way and transparently communicated to relevant internal and external stakeholders.

- ✓ There are many consultants providing help with risk assessments when time and resources are scarce. It is, however, not brain surgery, so try to internalize the learning and methodology, as a risk assessment needs to be repeated to ensure that the prorgamme stays relevant.

Organisation

When it comes to establishing a new Ethics and Compliance team, consider two basic questions: where to place the Ethics and Compliance department in the corporate hierarchy and how to staff the team. The organisational placement will be dependent on company characteristics such as industry, risk landscape and the need for a particular focus such as reversing historical misconduct. The board of directors should decide upon the organisational placement and ensure that the Chief Ethics and Compliance Officer (CECO) has a position of autonomy and access to an escalation mechanism. Independent access to the CEO and to the board is not only a powerful demonstration of leadership/tone from the top, but it is also a hallmark of effective compliance and adequate procedures as expected by regulators. Reporting lines are important, but it can be a "tick-in-the-box" concession with no real independent access. Other aspects of independence and genuine high-level support include airtime at management and board meetings as well as the possibility of private face-to-face meetings with the chairman of the board or one of its subcommittees. One should never underestimate how challenging it can be to be the one who challenges the status quo and how business deals have been structured, for example with the repeated use of questionable sales consultants or with sales persons who have been allowed to act without scrutiny. The rules may have been there, but they have not been enforced. A guaranteed source of friction is when existing rules suddenly are being enforced, consistently and persistently, it may take a while before the far off parts of the organisation realise that the rules are for real, and they are here to stay. The organisational structure should provide means for the CECO to voice concerns in confidence, alerting the board and executive management of the risks and issues that have to be tackled.

One of the first tasks of a CECO when building their organisation is to identify and capture relevant internal ethics and compliance resources that are scattered throughout the organisation. Internal expertise is crucial for a newly-established Ethics and Compliance team, especially if you join as CECO from the outside. There may be employees working in the procurement unit with third party compliance or in internal audit working with vendor audits and internal investigations. There may also be a unit working with risk management and internal controls, and some in the HR department working with organisational culture and values. An ethics and compliance organisation is a rather new phenomenon in European and Nordic companies, but the profession is on the rise and more and more companies are catching on. There is, however, still some confusion as to how to structure the organisation. Building an effective ethics and compliance programme is not about centralising all resources and building a standalone ethics and compliance organisation as a "line of defence" – it is about enabling the right business conduct throughout the business. It means ensuring that there are remedial action plans, which are closely monitored and that a compliance methodology of effectiveness and adequacy is followed. Most importantly, in the end, it is about enabling the company to build a culture of business ethics, integrity and honesty, supporting the friction and lifting the dilemmas to relevant levels of decision and responsibility in the organisation.

The ethics and compliance profession cuts across several disciplines such as legal, financial control, human resources, sustainability and risk management as well as specific conduct risks such as ABC, harassment, occupational health and safety, and security. Even if it is not necessary that the Ethics and Compliance department owns all the specific conduct risk compliance programmes, it may sometimes be an advantage. The Ethics and Compliance team can be better positioned to really push the agenda for the programme, as it should have access to power and authority and have fewer conflicting interests in the business operations and is not directly involved in the day-to-day business. The team can be advocates for what is right and ethical, while the legal team can often feel bound by legal interpretations and opinions and may have difficulties promoting ethical business practices. Finally, many of the ethics and compliance professionals are also specialists in one or several specific behavioural risks, such as ABC compliance, so you may as well kill two birds with one stone.

Coordination and sharing of information are key to successful compliance programmes overall; thus, you may want to organise the team to bridge, not reinforce, the corporate silos. Regardless of organisational structures, an Ethics and Compliance officer cannot be isolated in their own function but has to master cross-disciplinary cooperation as well as internal structures and silos.

Do not underestimate the silo structures and protection of turfs and positions in any organisation. We have experienced that management and boards often underestimate the disruptive and distortive force of turf-protection and silo structures. Executive management and the board are not exposed to the everyday politics, as they are normally above the turfs and silos. To drive true change it is crucial to understand and manage the turfs and the silos, and the Ethics and Compliance team can play an important role here, taking informal structures into account while at the same time providing cross-functional support and guidance.

The pitfall of compliance silos

You may ask yourself: how is it possible that a bank, for example, US-based Wells Fargo (agreed to being guilty of creating thousands of fake customer accounts) or Swedish Nordea (exposed for unethical behaviour in the so called "Panama Papers" scandal) can end up in such trouble with unethical maybe even unlawful behaviour when banks have huge compliance departments? Or pharma companies like GlaxoSmithKline (found guilty of bribery) whose operations normally have big departments called regulatory compliance or something similar.

Banks have very specific regulations related to their business, banking services, and pharma companies have very specific regulations related to their business, pharmaceutical products. Telecom businesses also have specific regulations that they need to comply with, related to the licenses and frequencies issued by the government. This is often called "regulatory compliance" and normally refers to an organisation's adherence to laws and regulations specifically relevant to its business. Not conduct risk and ethics and compliance as described in this book.

How is it possible that a company, such as Swedish Skanska can go through a terrible and haunting anti-competition scandal and then some years later find themselves in a bribery-scandal? Anti-competition is a conduct risk, as is bribery.

Well, these (repeated) scandals have, of course, many underlying reasons. It's best not to simplify events that many people have spent years analysing and coming to grips with. The point we want to make is that in many companies, where you have different exposures to different regulatory and legal/conduct risks, you may find built up "compliance silos" with skilled, educated and experienced people working with their specific programme, using different methodologies and processes. Not much cooperation and coordination goes on between the silos. As we strongly believe that the model of ethics and compliance, putting words into action and action into change, is applicable for all conduct risks, we also strongly believe in tearing down the silos. In our view, the duties of Ethics and Compliance as a function also includes ensuring identification, assessment, coordination, cooperation and consistency in managing all relevant conduct risks throughout the entire organisation.

Once you get the ethics and compliance framework in place in the organisation, including the risk assessments, trainings and other activities as well as engage many employees across the company, you will inevitably have some who are more interested and express an interest in supporting the programmes and efforts to build an ethical business culture. Make use of these supporters. Many companies establish "ethics ambassadors" or "ethics and compliance liaisons" to support aspects of rolling out the framework. It can be teaching different training modules, creating local ethics days or events, helping with questions and escalations or spreading the messages in other ways. Regardless of the tasks intended for the liaisons, it is important to have resources to support, engage and train them as well as to have aligned and consistent messages. It is also crucial to have doers within the business that can support and monitor the implementation in real time. An isolated corporate Ethics and Compliance team, with limited insight into the daily business, has little impact.

Competence and qualifications

Historically, lawyers have dominated the compliance profession. Our experience is that the ethics and compliance team should be staffed with various competencies, skills, qualifications and backgrounds. Compliance work is about understanding legal frameworks and ethics but also about the company governance, controls and financial processes, training, communication, investigations and diplomacy. It is also about understanding people and human reactions. The compliance team will benefit from a mix of disciplines and talents. In some circumstances, it may also be advantageous to hire an external compliance advisor who can challenge the structures, identify and assess internal resources and set up more efficient governance structures.

Our wish list for an Ethics and Compliance officer is long, and we realise that it may be mission impossible to find these qualities in one individual. We have therefore collected a list of qualities that we see as core qualities of the Ethics and Compliance team, as a team. We want to emphasise that ethics and compliance is not a quick fix, meaning just hiring the right person and then it is done. It will always be a team effort. This is so, certainly, within the ethics and compliance team, but more importantly between various functions and levels of the organisation. A compliance officer is not the perfect saint and spotless, but regardless has the task to uphold and protect the company's values and principles and to be the "stone in the shoe" when the temptation to cut corners enters the scene.

Our wish list – The super human Ethics and Compliance Officer

WHAT	WHY
Stamina and character to stand up when being questioned or challenged by business leaders and decision makers.	Even if many companies say that compliance is important and a way of doing business, there will be friction and dilemmas in the tug of war between different priorities in the business.
Persistent and uninfluenced, does not bend under pressure to massage the rules or force a decision, which may seem legal at the time, but may ultimately put the company or its stakeholders at great risk.	The company's best interest includes ensuring the best interest of both the current owners, management and board and the wider group of stakeholders, including society, environment and human rights.
Self-confident and willing to challenge yourself in the deep human desire to belong.	The job includes being prepared to bring friction and dilemmas up to relevant levels of authority in the company and to stand up for the company's values and principles, even when it sets you apart from the group and destroys the mood around the table.
Value driven – which may seem as a contradiction to some that relate compliance to rules and regulations (the policy police).	There are several dimensions to ethics and compliance, where the visible is set in policies and written rules and the invisible is the organisational psychology, pressures and power battles.
Be a change agent, analytical thinker and good collaborator.	In many respects, ethics and compliance is about change management, to change the corporate behaviour in the desired direction, which also requires analytical skills to understand the organisational state, needs and capacity to change.
A doer, who can interact with top management but at the same time, be present in the organisation.	Getting action on all levels.
A good and innovative communicator.	Getting the messages across.
A networker – both within the organisation and externally.	The role of the ethics and compliance officer may at times be frustrating and lonely, so strong support from the top levels in the company is a pre-requisite. We recommend belonging to professional groups and networks to get inspiration, learn and share. You will also gain credibility and confidence from engagement with your peers.

During my time at Telia Company, I had the opportunity to describe our Anti-Bribery and Corruption compliance programme in person during several meetings with the authorities. One meeting that was especially useful was the meeting with the [now former] Compliance Consultant at the US Department of Justice, Hui Chen. I will never forget the silence in the room when everybody waited for how she would open up the conversation, and I will also never forget her first question *"so tell me about who you have in your team?"*

One test of whether there is any action to the words is to be able to demonstrate that there are qualified, confident and sufficient resources within all relevant parts of the ethics and compliance organisation. If you are responsible for ethics and compliance, your job is to ensure that the management and board understand how much work actually is needed, and that you by no means are capable of doing this alone or in isolation. I was glad that the Board and management at Telia Company understood that we did not idly ask for resources and money and willingly approved a budget with at a minimum one E&C person in each critical risk country, including costs for certifications and adequate training for the entire team.

I encourage every Chief Ethics and Compliance officer to ask him or herself how they would feel to explain their organisation to a regulator. To have ethics and compliance liaisons in functions such as HR, Legal and Finance is great, but how much change will a person with multiple hats and 10 % dedicated to ethics and compliance be able to drive?

Ethics Committee

Ethics and compliance work is about action, and action generates friction. How should the company prioritise? Can we use a supplier for a helpdesk in India that has been accused of lax security but otherwise has great service and low prices? How shall we address this very important vendor in Turkey who refuses to disclose ultimate ownership? Escalation processes are necessary to ensure that different aspects of risk in decisions or actions are handled consistently. Reports on whistle-blowing cases and oversight as well as deliberations, consequence management and disciplinary actions, resulting out of internal investigations must go somewhere. The ethics and compliance team and programmes must have organised management interface and oversight and must manage the friction and dilemmas with necessary escalations. We recommend establishing *an Ethics Committee* with managers from the highest level to a management level that is reasonable for the size and structure of the company. Currently, we see boards establishing a subcommittee, specifically the board's ethics committee, representing the highest level in the company for oversight and escalations. Similar committees are needed at executive management level, regional management level and beyond, depending on size and structure of the company. There must never be any doubt as to conflicting interests in the ethics committees. If there is an investigation that needs considerations the relevant ethics committee is always one organisational layer above the highest-ranking officer involved in the matter. Sometimes with direct high-ranking reports, having two layers is preferable, assuring no real or perceived conflict of interest. In addition, it is a good idea to dedicate a slot at every management meeting at all levels for ethical dilemmas, difficult decisions and other relevant information from the ethics committee's work.

Keep in mind that the friction and dilemmas brought out in the open through the compliance programmes are signs of a healthy ethics and compliance programme, also when the friction reaches the executive management. Even without friction and dilemmas, there are many decisions to be made when introducing and implementing ethics and compliance programmes, requiring management attention and involvement. Policies and procedures must be decided upon, budgets approved, training and communication introduced, risk assessments carried out and shared. Moreover, there is a need for silos and hierarchies to be penetrated and information shared. It is hard to make room for these matters at the regular management meetings, and these topics typically tend to "fall off" the agenda as more interesting business matters are prioritised. Some CEOs have forced attention to the matters by introducing the item(s) first on the meeting agenda for management meetings. Another solution that we have had good experience from is establishing an additional leadership meeting (maybe extended with some functions such as internal audit, risk, control, sustainability if the regular management team is slimmed down) with a meeting agenda dedicated to risk, governance, responsible business, ethics and compliance.

Organisation – a quick checklist

- ✓ The CECO should have autonomy and independence, in other words direct and independent access to the CEO and executive management and a formalised independent reporting to the Board (or subcommittee).

- ✓ The E&C team should have the right competencies, diversity and seniority.

- ✓ Resources should be dimensioned to the level of risk.

- ✓ Resources should be both global and local to support management in high-risk jurisdictions, on country and regional level but all E&C officers should report to the CECO directly.

- ✓ The budget for E&C is one demonstration of the level of support and tone from the top.

- ✓ Regulatory authorities frequently ask about salary level for the CECO and the E&C team members as an easy measurement of the relevance of the function.

- ✓ The investigation team should be part of the E&C responsibility.

Policies and Procedures

Honestly, who gets overly excited talking about formal policies and instructions? Anyone else who is frustrated by being called "The Policy Police" and completely misunderstood for a "rules-based" person as opposed to the, much more interesting and meaningful, "values-based" person? We often hear about the values-based Code of Conduct (equals fun and approachable) as opposed to a rules-based Code of Conduct (boring and dogmatic). We are convinced that it is not rules *or* values – it is rules *and* values. Rules are a codification of your values.

For some people, policy work may also equal compliance work. They think along the lines of we need to get the policies and procedures in place, we need to demonstrate that we have "zero tolerance" for harassment or corruption, so we'll get a policy and some instructions drafted by a law firm, publish them on the intranet, maybe add some e-learning and awareness campaigns and consider "zero tolerance" implemented.

We also sometimes hear claims that policies on responsible business conduct are unnecessary. Everyone knows what is required – it is all just common sense. This may well be so, especially in a company with few employees and strong values, but there is need for clarity and guidance as the business environment becomes increasingly complex, global and transparent and with conflicting interests. It is not about being dogmatic or legalistic. It is about being clear and helpful and – sometimes – about making a statement. It is about providing clear and practical guidance to the employees across the organisation. What does "zero tolerance" mean in practice, and when is a gift no longer a gift but a bribe? Why is using an agent in one transaction acceptable when it is not ok in another transaction? Many Swedish and European companies are reluctant to introduce what they refer to as "American practices", with plenty of detailed regulations for everything, allowing little room for your own judgement. We do not argue that more policies and instructions will mean better compliance, but we do argue for clear and practical policies that can be applied globally and in a local context.

Codifying, building and strengthening your culture

The need for written documents, to explain what is required from each employee in different situations, will depend on several factors such as the number of employees, how widespread the organisation is and what type of business you are in. Behaving according to company values, "doing the right thing" may come naturally in a small organisation where everyone is located in the same office and every decision is visible. In general, however, you need more guidance than a statement. To do the right thing is not a catch phrase, you need to mean what you say and then put it into action. Written rules are codifications of our common values. What kind of company are we? What do we stand up for? What do we believe in? Who do we want to be? What is the right thing?

Policies and the procedures are only the starting point, but you do need them and more often than not we have seen our colleagues welcoming such guidance. Maybe you have done your conduct risk assessment and have decided what topics of corporate conduct you need to cover. Now you need to understand the company's position on the topic and what policies are needed to make that position clear. Every company is different. They use different names (policies, instructions, guidelines, directives) and have different delegations of authority but a policy is normally the written format of the words spoken by the highest level of governance in the company, the board. The next level of governance, the leadership at executive or similar level, issues instructions as a written format of their words to explain further what the policy requires from the employees. Maybe the company also allows for additional guidelines issued by different operationally responsible managers, to break down the details even further. This is the hierarchy of rules in many companies we have worked with; however, what you call documents of written rules in different details and levels in companies varies. The most important point here is that these documents are binding rules of conduct in the company. We will refer to these documents as "policies/instructions". You will also find documents such as "position papers" or "statements", describing a general direction or general opinion on a specific matter but without any more detail or rules for behaviour. A position paper can be useful as a first step towards creating more specific rules and guidelines, policies/instructions, on the subject matter. A position paper may be a way for the board to push the organisation into action. However, if the position paper sits around for too long without any further action, it might turn into empty words and an embarrassment, of talking but not walking. In addition to the policies/instructions, there may be formalised processes, enabling practical implementation of the policy/instruction, such as a description of an escalation process for decisions.

In a highly regulated industry, for example, the car industry or a bank, there is bound to be a lot of focus on legal and regulatory compliance requirements and many rules and procedures. Hopefully, in such businesses, there is a quality department or a regulatory compliance department that is responsible for this compliance work, specific for the industry. If the ethics and compliance department also has this responsibility, there is a high likelihood that the wider

concept of corporate conduct, understanding the external context, your conduct risks and business ethics will be pushed aside.

In formulating "the right thing to do" for the business, you may have to consider a broader view than strictly following the law – legal compliance.

You may want to consider that laws are seldom black or white, but outline a grey zone, where taking underlying common norms into consideration will protect the company from wrongdoing. Having done an assessment of the company's context and conduct risks, you will have good understanding of what norms and ethical expectations should be considered for your own framework of rules.

The board of directors decides the path and this translates into policies/instructions, processes and guidelines. Just make sure, without a doubt, that what you say and what you do is the same. Do not make a claim or prescribe in the rules to the employees something that you are not willing to hold on to when push comes to shove. Do not break your own rules. Double standards are confusing and will deteriorate the entire programme and put the company at risk of conduct failure. Having said this, there are many reasons why there should be exceptions to your own rules. The company's Supplier / Business Partner Code of Conduct can set high standards, and you may agree that it is reasonable to give a supplier a reasonable grace period to catch up. In some situations, you may also have to make exceptions from important rules. It can be a matter of more important business considerations. In making exceptions, there needs to be very clear escalations and transparent decisions by the correct management level and authority in the company. Keep in mind that every unclear, incomprehensible or simply wrong exception will undermine the rules and the work morale of those whose job it is to upkeep the rules and support the company in staying out of trouble and building the corporate conduct and culture.

Too few …?

At the corporate level, we often hear that we have to trust our colleagues to do the right thing and that it is common sense, but "common sense" is an unreliable source of guidance, particularly in global business where individuals have different understandings of what is common and what is sense. In our travels to operations in locations where corruption is penetrating the society, our colleagues there have asked for more policies, more rules and clear practical scenarios to support them in applying "common sense" in their daily challenging reality.

However, in some organisations, typically the public sector but also in other large corporations, there is – in our view – an over-reliance on written rules and guidelines. Whenever something goes wrong, more rules and guidelines are issued to prevent the same wrongdoing from happening again. Additional "layers of control" may also be proposed

Or too many …?

for improvement and remedial action to fix the problem. As we will come back to in Chapter Six below, added rules and layers of control may not be the solution to fix the problem at all. Totally stripping leaders and the organisation of trust will not exactly empower people to think for themselves and to develop a sense of what is right or wrong; thus, it will not build a culture of ethics.

The bottom line is that you will have to find a balance between too few and too many, depending on the organisation and the situation. However, a compliance programme without proper documentation of the common rules is not effective. You have to ensure that relevant topical policies/instructions are consistently drafted, anchored and approved throughout the group.

We have zero tolerance for corruption – in more specific words …

Coming back to statements such as "We have zero tolerance for corruption". This is a very high-level statement, and it requires quite a few additional words to make it possible for employees to understand. Some examples of additional information include:

- a policy and instruction on anti-corruption,
- a policy on money laundering,
- instructions on gifts and hospitality,
- instructions on interactions with government officials,
- instructions on sponsorship, donations and philanthropic contributions,
- instructions on use of agents, distributors and similar third parties for the sale and promotion of the company's products and services.

In addition, it can include:

- instructions on internal investigations,
- instructions on corrective and disciplinary actions,
- procurement and third party screening policy and
- instructions on a M&A policy.

The policies/instructions in the ABC programme create content and texture to what you mean by "zero tolerance".

Policy Administration

Even if the responsibility for the specific conduct risk lies outside of the ethics and compliance team, there are important administrative considerations and coordinating tasks that the ethics and compliance team should do or otherwise ensure. One suggestion is to appoint one member of the team to be responsible for policy administration and ensure that this person has patience and is a good "corporate diplomat", ensuring that all corporate policy documents are consistently drafted, properly anchored and finally, approved at the right level. It is tempting to use a specialist, such as a law firm that will provide excellent template documents. There is nothing wrong with that, just make sure to go through the documents with relevant stakeholders. Internal buy-in is also an exercise of awareness and spending time at this stage will make the implementation and transition from words into actions smoother.

You want to have polices that are relevant for your organisation and that everyone can embrace.

Some companies have too many policies/instructions and some too few; some date back to the industrial revolution and some are new, as new employees have arrived and started to engage in a specific area of conduct risk. It is therefore also good advice to regularly make a list of all policies and instructions and evaluate if all are needed and relevant. We also really like the idea of having one person, who understands how to communicate clearly and without complicated legal or technical lingo, editing all policies/instructions after the owner has written them, to ensure the same corporate feel of the documents and prevent use of unnecessarily complicated language.

In a bigger organisation it is a probably a good investment to use a policy management tool to keep track of the documents and ensure distribution to all relevant employees. A policy management tool enables you to document which individuals have read, signed-off and committed to the policy. What is not documented, did not happen; some companies that have ended up in trouble with the law for questionable conduct by one of their employees have been helped by being able to demonstrate, among other things, that the relevant policy/instruction had been sent to and signed off by the employee in question. It is also important to ensure that the critical policies/instructions are available in the relevant local languages. If your ethics and compliance program at some point would be subject to regulatory scrutiny, they will surely ask whether the applicable policy document was available in the language of the country where the misconduct happened. And further a regulator will likely ask you for assurance of how you know that the relevant employees actually were aware of the corporate rules. A policy on the corporate intranet that no one has read, or would not understand if they happened to find it, will not protect the company …

There may be certain conduct risks that cut across different topics, such as human rights and children's rights. The UNICEF

Children's Rights and Business Principles provide guidance for businesses in respecting children and their rights, and the company may want to consider including these principles in the different topical policies/instructions.

Telia Code of Responsible Business Conduct – rules can be fun as well

A Code of Conduct is an umbrella document. An umbrella providing easy access and easier understanding of the internal framework of rules and requirements the company has for how to behave at work. For once, we agree with the communications folks, "It's all about communication". A Code of Conduct should be enjoyable to read, modern and accessible. As an umbrella, the code needs to stand on firm ground of policies/instructions, otherwise there is no real substance to the Code of Conduct. The Telia Company Code of Responsible Business Conduct, "Don't do this at work" was launched in 2016; it is easily accessible in paper and electronic form, both internally and externally. It is fun and easy to read and has links to underlying policies/instructions.

DON'T DO THIS AT WORK

dontdothisatwork.teliacompany.com

What applies in your own company should also apply to your third parties and others representing the company. Many companies have a separate code of conduct for third parties. At Telia Company, the Supplier Code of Conduct sets out requirements for suppliers and is accompanied by specific internal guidance for how and when it is possible to make exceptions to the requirements and how to follow-up on agreed action plans.

Policies and Procedures – a quick checklist

- ✓ Decide and document the hierarchy and governance of written rules for the company; policies, instructions, guidelines.

- ✓ Organize, clean up and structure them to make them accessible and readable.

- ✓ Decide what is a reasonable level of rules in the company – what is too many and what is too few?

- ✓ The internal framework of rules needs to be administrated, updated and kept alive. That will probably not happen unless someone is responsible for this task.

- ✓ Take a look at your Code of Conduct – do people read it? A Code of Conduct is, in our view, an umbrella document, a communications tool to make the internal framework of rules accessible and understandable to the relevant stakeholders.

Training and Communication

Once you have codified the corporate view and expectations on conduct into formal rules, you need to make sure that everybody who should know about them are aware, as well as understands them and can apply them in practice. Many of us celebrate when we have issued a policy/instruction or a Code of Conduct. Celebration of achievements is always a good idea, however, the efforts required for creating a policy/instruction or a Code of Conduct cannot be compared to the time and effort required to actually implement it in practice. We usually say that it only takes you ten seconds to say that you have written a policy and that everybody is now trained, but it takes substantial effort to actually do that in practice. A successful compliance programme is one that

How many times have e-learning courses been clicked through, while doing emails on another device?

is able to drive change from within, through appealing to personal values and beliefs and creating an environment where the right behaviour is the norm. It is not only about e-learning courses and intranet articles, it is about "calibrating the internal compass" of each and every employee towards the right behaviour.

Having said that, in building a culture of awareness and doing the right thing, training and continued education are fundamental. Once out of school, you really want to consider yourself as being educated, but as we all know deep down, that is unfortunately not true. We are also quite busy during a workday with emails, meetings and day-to-day business, so there is not a lot of time to reflect, think and develop new knowledge and awareness. How many times have e-learning courses been clicked through, while doing emails on another device? This is not a meaningful exercise and really is a waste of time and money. But how do you do it then, when you have 30,000 employees and no access to troops of trainers and have to fight for airtime with the employees.

The power of why – Fear is a blunt weapon

As the famous Ted talker Simon Sinek[22] does, we also believe in the power of why, although some experts have argued that one should not start with *why* but with *who*. Well, for us, and in relation to corporate conduct, it does not really matter if you consider why or who first as both lead us towards the understanding that the rules are based on considerations of ethics, moral and common values. Never underestimate the intelligence of your colleagues. No one likes to be patronised or waste time. Your colleagues are educated and intelligent adults so it is important to maintain a level of quality of the content and format of the training in order to keep it fresh, new and interesting. Explain why an anti-corruption programme is important, not just because the company is in crisis mode or risks

22   https://www.youtube.com/watch?v=u4ZoJKF_VuA

prosecution and high fines for bribery but because the effects of corruption in the world and its impact on society and human rights are devastating. Corruption destroys fair value distribution, hinders democracy, enables all sorts of crimes and acts of terror, it prevents schools and hospitals from being built and it hurts the poor the most. It contributes to the increased gap between those who have and those who have not. That is who is the ultimate victim and why it is also illegal under several legislations, which if violated can be costly and sometimes also result in personal criminal liability. It is also unethical and exposes the company to huge risk of reputational damage. It destroys the moral fibre of the company, and where bribery is present, fraud and theft are ever-present, which are more damaging to the company than any gain achieved from a bribe. This is why.

Compliance can be driven out of fear: fear of reputational damage, fear of prosecution and personal disgrace, fear of very high criminal penalties and debarment. Fear as a tool to build the ethical core and exercise the ethical muscles to strengthen a culture of business ethics is, however, a blunt tool. Ultimately, we want to have people who do the right thing because it is right and not because they are afraid of prosecutors, journalists, jail or fines.

To the left above is a global mapping of human rights risks, an index developed by Verisk-Maplecroft. It shows that in 110 out of 198 countries, there is a high- or extreme risk of human rights violations. You might want to compare the map on the left with the map on the right, showing

Transparency International Corruption Perception Index. It is a useful pedagogic way of showing that corruption, at its core, is really a human rights problem and a way of explaining why it is such a big global problem that we should all want to fight corruption, not because we are afraid but because we value human rights and values and share a responsibility to do things right.

How to structure your training efforts – some lessons learned

When

Make a plan for your training efforts, both to prioritise your time but also the time of others. One needs to be respectful of everyone's time and make efforts to coordinate different training modules as well as training for the different compliance programmes. In the plan for training and education, be sure to include the aspect of who needs this training in the course of doing their job.

Who

We have learned the hard way that not all employees need to be trained on all internal rules and procedures. As an example, the rules on money laundering are very important but a limited group of people are typically exposed to these risks. Thus, in addressing these employees, you might want to build a whole block of related training such as anti-corruption and detecting fraud. Another example includes employees in the factory, who most often are not exposed to anti-trust aspects of doing business but much more so to health and safety risks. The most important thing is not that *all* employees have completed the training – but that all the *relevant* employees have a detailed understanding of what they should know. Therefore, a general "one size fits all" Code of Conduct training may not be as effective as you think.

Some trainings are obligatory for some groups of employees and some can be voluntary; plan this carefully so as not to overload the employees. One company impressed us, as it was not possible to file travel expenses before you did the training on business entertainment, hospitality and gifts, a clever way of gently forcing those who need to know the rules to complete the training.

How
Integrated training – whenever it is possible, try to integrate compliance training in other educational activities the company offers its leaders and employees. This reinforces the message that business practices an compliance wth laws, rules and ethical expectations is not a side-show but each and everyone's daily responsibility – business as usual.

Combined activities – sometimes it can be very effective to do campaigns where you combine training with other activities. Putting up signs for people to hold the handrail in the stairwell, while at the same time rolling out training on safety enforces the message of the trainings. Having posters in the offices on speaking up and articles on the intranet on the effects of retaliation or a movie with the CEO encouraging an open culture, at the same time as providing training in your new Code of Conduct can also be a good combination to enforce the message.

E-learning courses – most compliance programmes include some form of e-learning. E-learning is an effective way to reach out to a large target group at the same time and also to be able to record who has "clicked through" the module. Nowadays, there are some very intelligent interactive e-learning courses, which are engaging and have a structure that prevents the "pupil" from mindlessly clicking through it. Choose wisely and for important topics, make sure that the training effort does not stop with e-learning but is also complemented with other forms of training. There is also e-learning available that initially starts with the participant selecting, for example work responsibilities, seniority and location and then the training is automatically tailored to the profile of that particular person.

Face-to-face training – we believe that, without a doubt, different In-Real-Life (IRL) training is the best and most effective way to reach out to your colleagues. It enables intelligent and active dialogue, instant feedback and also requires high quality and relevant content, focus and engagement. Keeping in mind that the content relevant for one group of colleagues may be less relevant for another group, be prepared to tailor the content to the specific group.

In a face-to-face training session, you can have classroom training, which is really more education-type training, teaching your colleagues a topic such as corruption or conflict minerals. This is sometimes necessary, especially for the high risk groups that should have a more in-depth understanding of the "what and why". For other groups or as a next level in the training, ethical dilemma discussions and workshops are more effective and engaging ways to instil increased awareness. In creating ethical dilemmas, make sure to number them and keep stock of them. Do not make dilemmas easy with clear-cut answers; it should reflect that it is a dilemma (and not a test) and that some thinking needs to take place (and that there may be no "right" answer). Make sure that you are available for informal discussions after the training as our experience is that the sensitive questions will not be asked in the group, it is also not unlikely that a discussion after a training will prompt an internal investigation.

Train the trainers – if you use more than one person for training, you may want to invest in your trainers so that they can all convey the same message and respond consistently to questions. We recommend train-the-trainer sessions and building a compliance champion network in the company, enabling more face-to-face training and building the bank of ethical dilemmas. In building this internal competence, we have found that it pays to sometimes bring in an external lecturer to spin things around a bit and make the topic more interesting. In some sessions, for example, when you have the opportunity to have the attention of the leadership in the company, you might want to invest a little extra and have an external lecturer, who brings his or her own special flavour to the topic, join you to talk about ethics, safety or diversity. The leaders should, of course, also want to listen to their own ethics and compliance officers who should be able to address all layers, from board level and out in the company.

Repetition is the mother of all learning – especially in a corporation where people come and go. When introducing a new Code of Conduct or a new anti-bribery-corruption programme, you pretty much exhaust yourself in the training exercise and the thought of doing it again feels daunting. However, the journey is never ending, so new and improved training will always be part of an effective programme. We have done so many training sessions in small groups, big groups, web-based groups, using dilemma-based and classroom-type training – and we have come to accept that change takes time and each person needs to feel that the change comes from within. While building knowledge, understanding and acceptance, you are also building culture.

Test the effectiveness – great advice (thank you Hui Chen @HuiChen-Ethics) is to, before a training session, send out some questions on the topic to the participants. Then, after some months repeat the exercise to see what has actually stuck from the training. Don't send out the questions too soon after the training, you don't want to test short term memory but rather test if the training has had a lasting impact.

Fundamentally, "training" is about engaging in a dialogue with the organisation – make sure that you share your own lessons learned and avoid a one-way lecture-type situation. A dialogue typically is a two-way communication, you reaching out with your message but also of you listening. A great deal of listening happens through analysing the cases from your speaking up and whistle-blowing channels. You need to listen to the organisation and understand where the weaknesses and vulnerabilities are and weave these into the dialogue through your training programmes and activities. By analysing your whistleblowing cases and reported non-compliance issues you will understand whether your training efforts are effective. It is no use spending time and money on extensive roadshows if whistleblowing cases show that people who are aware of the basic rules still break them. In that case it is perhaps not about more training but time to take a step back and re-assess your internal context, your culture and root causes. Perhaps the problem is that decisions are constantly being made which undermines all the training efforts.

As we firmly believe that it is only through employees, and leaders' decisions and actions that you can really be successful in driving a lasting change in behaviour and creating a culture of "doing the right thing", training in aspects of decision-making is vital. Decision makers should be trained in understanding that making the right decision may not be intuitive and at times may be very hard. It is important to identify and reflect upon the factors that one is not aware of but that will subconsciously affect decisions, such as the normalisation of misconduct and silent acceptance of non-compliance or how lack of diversity and inclusion may breed misconduct and negatively affect the quality of decisions. How fear and pressure due to groupthink, time constraints or hierarchical thinking ("my boss has signed off so it is probably ok") affect us so that even good people can end up making bad decisions.

The emperor is naked - ethical blindness and ethical dilemmas

 We have worked together with Professor and Doctor Guido Palazzo to shed light on what he refers to as "ethical blindness", how you can be influenced by factors that may momentarily "blind" you so as to prevent you from doing the right thing, making the right choice or decision. Good people (like yourself) can make bad decisions when put in difficult situations.

While we normally believe that bad people do bad things, the idea of ethical blindness highlights the fact that everyone has the potential to be involved in unethical/illegal behaviour. This behaviour is not driven by the character of the person (as we normally believe) but by the power of the context in which someone makes a decision. The situation can be stronger than the person and stronger than reason. Influenced by the context – organisational pressure (maybe fear of failure or ridicule) or situational pressure (maybe time pressure, maybe group pressure, maybe authority pressure) – we start to perceive the world through a filter or through a tunnel, preventing us from seeing clearly or outside of the tunnel. We can become momentarily "blind". There are many different physiological experiments and theories on this (for example Palazzo's article on ethical blindness published in the Journal of Business Ethics) if you want to learn more. We like the story about the vain and repressive emperor, who created fear and surrounded himself with yea-sayers, ending up being ridiculed, naked and defrauded by tricksters, because this old tale reminds us that nothing is ever really new …

Some ethical dilemmas in practice

Below is a collection of ethical dilemmas. Remember that the most important thing with dilemmas is not necessarily the solution but the discussion.

- Your company is sending managers for a week of product testing at a supplier. The purpose of the testing is to sign off and give final approval that the product is developed according to your company's requirements. You participate in the test team from your department and spend long days on the tests. There are some issues with the system that the supplier has developed and there are doubts as to whether you should sign-off or not. At the end of the week, the supplier wants to invite the whole test team from your company to an ice hockey game as a way to thank them for a good week and all their efforts. What do you do? The supplier also wants to give the managers in the test team a personal gift card. Should they accept the gift card?

- Your manager has a great house with a pool in Italy. You are invited to come and spend a weekend with your spouse and kids in June. Is that okay? Your manager has left the company and is now your "former manager" and friend instead, working as a senior consultant with his own business. Is it okay to go now?

- Your former manager, that has left the company and now works as a CEO of a competitor, and as such has access to tickets in the private box at Wimbledon for the semi-finals. As he is not able to go, he invites you to use the box for family and friends. Is this okay?

- Your company has recently signed a very large business deal with a state-owned company in Nigeria. During the celebration dinner you overhear a conversation between your local spare parts reseller and your manager. You do not catch the entire conversation but hear something about informal customer discussions and pricing information of competitors. At first you do not think it is such a big deal, your manager has received the same training as you and this deal was critical to hit the quarterly targets. But on your way home you start to hesitate, what should you do with the information?

Is the patient rejecting the medicine?

Building awareness and culture with the wrong people in leadership and management is not going to work and too often you see companies investing in extensive training efforts but it becomes a "tick in the box" exercise because you have the wrong people on board. Sometimes, it is therefore necessary to tear down and destroy a culture before you can build something new. We know of a company which established a business in Russia and some years later had such grave problems of corruption, bribes, fraud and retaliation that the whole venture more or less had to close down and the company needed to start all over again from the beginning. Everybody had to go, a rather dramatic decision as surely not all employees were part of the corrupt culture, but separating the good from the bad would have taken too long and with the risks involved it was the right decision. In another country and with a different company, maybe the risk would have been manageable during the time it takes to investigate, remediate, discipline and correct. A general observation is however that it is easy to disregard dismantling of the old, especially if you are part of something new in the company, where you tend to under-evaluate the impact of the old and over-evaluate the impact of the new.

Training and Communication – a quick checklist

✓ Remember that fear may be a blunt weapon (fear of criminal sanctions and adverse media attention) and understanding why (how corruption is cheating in business and a global menace undermining human rights, democracy and our efforts to fulfil, for example, the UN sustainable development goals) can be very powerful in working.

✓ Mix it up. Make it interesting. Use dilemmas, preferably from the company itself.

✓ All training is not relevant for all. And employees have limited time. Spend time planning and coordinating training.

✓ Training should also include aspects that are common for all conduct risks, such as retaliation, whistleblowing, inferences.

✓ Spend some time and effort training the trainers.

✓ Make sure that corporate conduct and ethics and compliance training is also part of leadership training increasing awareness of the grey zone and human aspects such as, for example, ethical blindness.

✓ Keep participant records from all trainings.

Speaking Up and Investigations

A central element of implementing a culture of transparency and integrity is engaging in a dialogue. And rarely does a constructive and open dialogue just happen. You actively need to promote a culture of transparency – talking about issues, friction, mistakes, challenges and lessons learned. Problematise. Promote a culture where raising concerns are the norm and where issues can be addressed before they become failures. You need mechanisms to understand when the efforts you put into building compliance and a culture of business ethics, integrity and transparency is not working and to understand whether there is misconduct that undermines the efforts. A whistle-blowing channel for anonymous reporting is one such important mechanism. Information on the table about misconduct happening in the organisation will force a discussion. There are many great external providers of whistle-blowing solutions that are easy to access, both internally and externally using modern technology, enabling reporting from employees as well as externals, such as vendors and consultants all over the world.

Most of us think we are straightforward, honest, easy going, accessible and have integrity and guts. That may well be true, but in the corporate context, group behaviour, fear and pressure can muzzle us and make us conveniently agreeable or deaf in response to disturbing signals. It is easy to say that: leaders should engage in a dialogue with subordinates and colleagues; we should listen to the organisation, notice red flags and inconsistencies or signs of behavioural failure and have the capabilities to tackle these issues within the "normal" operational processes or escalations to superiors; and that it is everybody's responsibility to speak up when we see something is wrong. In reality, though, we know this is hard. The one who speaks up is commonly the outlier. We do not want to speak up, act or blow the whistle when we see something that is wrong; rather, we want to conform and be part of the group. In reality, we too often shut our eyes to wrongdoing and think it is someone else's responsibility. In a recent study, conducted in the Nordics, it appears that a majority of employees who has witnessed some misconduct decide not to do anything. Almost 25 % of managers do the same; nothing. [23]

Employees leaving the company may be more inclined to speak up about matters that have been bothering them. Since they are leaving anyway, the risk of retaliation is lower. However, some power structures reach far beyond the company walls, so also after having left the company it is still important to protect the integrity of the employee. From not only an ethics and compliance point of view, it should be mandatory to conduct exit-interviews with all employees who leave the company. We realise that scarce resources

23   www.nordicbusinessethics.com

may make this difficult, but there may be ways to get around the limitations. One alternative would be to, as a first step, do the interview via an email with a short pre-formulated questionnaire and only if this raises red flags or the employee expresses a wish to continue the interview with the ethics and compliance team, there would be a follow-up interview.

Standing alone

In 2012, Eyal Press, an American journalist published a book called "Beautiful Souls". Reading this book was the defining experience that finally tipped the scales for me to abandon my career as a corporate lawyer and focus only on ethics and compliance. Press describes four different persons in very different circumstances but who have one thing in common. They have stood out and done the right thing when everyone else around them failed. Paul Grüninger was a Swiss border police commander, who broke the law and falsified the stamp in the passports of Jewish refugees, to pre-date the day when the law that closed the Swiss borders for Jews was introduced in 1938. With this simple measure, hundreds of Jews could pass through Grüninger's passport control booth when others were turned away at other border controls. He was discovered after a while, of course. He lost his job and never got a new one. After he died, his hometown raised a statue of him in thankful memory. His daughter remembers him repeating the answer "I could do nothing else", when asked what made him do it. Grüninger was not an activist or rebel. He had a family to provide for. He took his job and his oath to uphold the law and serve his country seriously.

Eyal Press writes about Grüninger to find an explanation about what made Grüninger this unlikely and almost unwilling hero. He also writes about a Serb who saved the lives of Croats by lying about their ethnic identity, about an elite Israeli soldier who refused to serve in the occupied territories, and a whistle-blower who exposed corrupt bankers. He writes about ordinary people who did the right thing and paid a high personal price. So why did they do it? This is, of course, a very relevant and interesting question, which Press tries to find an answer to in his book, but for me the question I asked myself was, would I have done the right thing or would I be among "the others"? Chances are I would not have done the right thing. My vision would most probably have been clouded or impaired by the strong forces of fear, or group or hierarchical pressure.

The dilemma of speaking truth to power and being killed as the messenger

In conveying an uncomfortable message, you run a high risk of becoming uncomfortable yourself, where instead of focusing on the uncomfortable problem, people may question you. The risk of the messenger being killed is ancient knowledge, so it is not so strange that we tend to avoid such a situation. We do not want to put difficult dilemmas or problems with no obvious solution on the table. We want to bring solutions and clarity. To bypass your direct manager and take a problem to the next level is suicidal. The information flow upwards in most organisations is restricted – for good reasons, there is a limit to how much information any person, however intelligent, can absorb and handle. However, in the process of deciding what and how matters should be raised and presented at the next level, there is high risk that vital information gets lost due to our aversion to problematise and raise difficult and uncomfortable matters to the next level. Every organisational layer is a filter. This is especially effective for filtering out information that is uncomfortable, problematic or worrisome. Speaking truth to power is hard. Even as compliance professionals, who are used to bringing uncomfortable messages, we sometimes cringe when we have to and find ourselves trying to appease the audience by sugarcoating the message in one way or another or by undertaking to personally solve the situation at hand, to ease the irritation in the room.

Not only do we have strong mechanisms of group or hierarchical pressure or of "killing the messenger", we also have an inherent, strong dislike and distrust of people who "snitch", and you do not exactly win any popularity contest by speaking up. If at least all whistle-blowers were honest people with noble causes, it would be so much easier for us to write and speak about whistle-blowers and non-retaliation. Alas, not all whistle-blowers have noble intentions; we have had whistle-blowers that clearly come forward driven by greed or revenge. Not at all pleasant people, but as it transpired after investigations, their allegations turned out to be true. However, most people who come forward to "do the right thing" are genuinely concerned that something is amiss and care deeply about their company and workplace. They often speak of how proud they are of the company they work for and how they feel it is somehow being misused or changing for the worse.

> **Conveying an uncomfortable message is difficult, and you run a high risk of becoming uncomfortable yourself.**

Fear of retaliation

Sometimes the internal corporate context deters people from speaking up, maybe a bossy boss, strong group pressure or strong conflicting goals. Sometimes, the external context is deterring. If you, for example, have operations in highly complex and corrupt markets, the company values and norms may differ significantly from what your colleagues experience after work. At work, it is not allowed to offer an expensive gift to win business. But privately, they have to give expensive gifts so their children are accepted to a particular school or get relevant medical attention. To offer a bribe is ordinary and expected. Many of us working at the head office of a global company live in an environment where the external context provides security if we would challenge the system or our employer. In highly corrupt countries, there are no guarantees for what might happen if you get off on the wrong foot with the wrong people. When promoting internal whistle-blowing channels, you must also provide security for your colleagues. Security that the investigation is handled with confidentiality and professionalism. Security that any attempt at retaliation will be firmly dealt with. This is so much easier in theory than in practice, but vital for the success of your compliance programme.

The most important factor that deters people from speaking up is that they are afraid of retaliation. Retaliation can be many things: big things such as being bypassed for a promotion or smaller things such as ending up less popular in the group. Retaliation can go on for a short period but can also continue and worsen into systematic mistreatment of a person who in the end finds her or himself forced to leave the company. It is important to keep in mind that we are all creatures who want to be well liked and respected. We rely on the group and to be part of the group is important for survival. This is true even in the corporate context. The difficulties of speaking up, retaliation, humiliation and sometimes, ultimately, finding yourself unemployed have led to legislation in the US, where authorities (the DOJ, OSHA and IRS[24], for example) can reward whistle-blowers who come forward with an allegation that later is substantiated and punished. As the fines for corporate wrongdoing are very high in the US, so too are the whistle-blower rewards, sometimes millions of dollars. In Europe, authorities reject this approach and although companies sometimes discuss having a system of rewards to recognise people who speak up, we do not know of any company that has actually implemented this.

There are many examples of where a huge corporate crisis is initiated by a whistle-blower who decides to go external, most effectively to media. You would want to think this is normally an employee or a vendor who is disloyal, disgruntled or have other reasons to damage the company. Sometimes that is the case, but in majority of these cases, the person has actually tried to speak up within the organisation but not received any relevant attention or action on their claims/allegations.

---

24   DOJ: Department of Justice, OSHA: US Occupational Security and Health Administration and IRS: Internal Revenue Service.

Many "whistle-blower" cases do not warrant more attention than acknowledgement of receipt and a polite explanation as to why the matter will be closed without further action taken, but whistle-blowing may also be the first step in a lengthy investigation into fraud and corruption. Whistle blowing can also be an indication of there potentially being conflicting goals within the organisation, or that we may drive the wrong behaviour through incentives, or that the corporate processes have failed. It is also an indication that managers have not been able to engage in effective dialogue with colleagues and subordinates; thus, to blow the whistle is a last resort to speak up about something which concerns the person.

Sometimes the concerns raised by the whistle-blower are unfounded and, as infuriating as it may seem for many managers who are used to managing and taking action, one action that is not allowed, is to try to find out who the whistle-blower may be.

Barclays CEO disciplined.

CEO, Jes Staley, at Barclays allegedly used the bank's security function to discover who wrote letters to Members of the Board of the bank. The letters in question alleged all sorts of dirt related to another high-level employee hired to help Staley turn Barclays around and were treated as a whistle-blowing matter by the Barclays compliance team and were investigated and subsequently closed as not substantiated. Staley probably had good intentions and the whistle-blower did not, but in trying to disclose the identity of the whistle-blower, Staley breached internal rules on whistle-blowing as well as bank regulations. The Board felt

obliged to punish the otherwise trusted CEO by clawing back 500.000 GBP of his bonus and issue a formal warning, but if that was not enough, UK regulatory authorities have also subsequently investigated the matter and Staley has been fined 642.430 GBP for "failure to act with due skill, care and diligence.

Investigations

Another important factor to deter people from speaking up is stated as "nothing happens anyway, so why would I expose myself to the uncomfortable consequences of speaking up". It is a fair statement and puts a spotlight on the importance of high quality internal investigations. And high quality investigations put the spotlight on remediation, consequence management, disciplinary and corrective actions as well as transparency.

When someone has dug deep into their conscience and reported suspect or strange behaviour that could turn out to be a real breach against the Code of Conduct or the law, it is very damaging for the whistle-blowing process, the compliance programme and the trust in the company if the report and the reporter are not taken seriously and professionally. It is equally damaging, if the whistle-blowing report turns out to be a real wrongdoing and the subsequent handling and investigations are not done professionally. The case may be closed due to insufficient evidence, inadequate investigation or lack of attention to the matter. This will speak against the company later, if or when, the case pops up again, in media or at the prosecutor's desk.

Conducting qualified, swift and independent internal investigations on allegations of fraud, corruption, conflict of interest or embezzlement with high integrity is a very important part of effective compliance. It is also a very difficult, generally thankless and lonely job and requires special skills and stamina. Having the right person in internal investigations is somewhat like having your own investigative journalist on board. The job requires extensive experience and an extraordinary sense of integrity. A good investigator is hard to find. An investigator needs to be curious, patient and persistent; he or she needs to have the capabilities to find information from various sources and be able to conduct difficult interviews. While doing all this, the investigator must be well organised and keep records of all incoming, ongoing and closed cases, ensuring that there is always adequate documentation. A good investigator is able to make judgement calls and understand when putting additional efforts into the investigation will be a waste of time, but also understand when to keep pressing and not give up. In addition, there are regulatory issues that need to be understood and complied with; for example, the concerns of privacy in internal investigations are increasing, at least in Europe, where it is important that personal identification be removed from records and archives.

Special investigations are not the same as an audit

An Internal Audit is a very important function for assurance in any company or organisation. It is, however, not the same as an investigation. I can safely say this, as I myself have worked with both. Investigations of suspected fraud, corruption, bribes, money laundering and theft require a particular skillset and require going beyond looking at processes and controls. An auditor can, of course, become an investigator just like any other educated person, but is not an investigator by default. It may be tempting to close an internal investigation due to "lack of evidence", or because the internal process was followed, the contract was approved by the right person, the expense was reported in the project cost sheet and the external auditor has signed off the statutory accounts. But digging deeper you may find serious misconduct despite compliance with internal processes. From an audit perspective the suspected misconduct may not be material, however it may say something very critical about your culture and respect for compliance. Fraud schemes are usually well crafted and require equally well-crafted procedures to unlock. Internal audit is however one of the best friends of special investigations and can assist and complement many investigations, as they have a great helicopter view of the business as well as knowledge of financial systems and formal processes.

During a sensitive investigation, there are also many interfaces inside and outside of the organisation that must be dealt with;

moreover, information must, to a certain extent, be provided to, for example, the board, the ethics committee, internal audit, external audit, communications department, media, relevant managers, the whistle-blower, legal department, external lawyers and maybe even the police and prosecutor. Of course, it may not be the investigator's job to deal with all these requests for information, but the source of information comes from the investigator, so she or he needs to understand how to deal with sensitive information and be firm when it is too early to share information or when there is no new information to share.

To ensure that the process around internal investigations is formalised, we recommend issuing a corporate policy or instruction. This document, increasingly required by law, sets out the rights and obligations of the employees and informs them what happens when a whistle-blowing report has been made. In this instruction, you specify the process, roles, responsibilities and documentation. In this way, it will be clear how the investigations are managed and handled, and you will be able to retain external consultants when you have a time-consuming investigation or several parallel investigations while maintaining a consistent internal routine. There is a lot of pressure to see the results of an investigation, and a professional investigation should be timely and not linger over a long period, which is hurtful for the people involved and irritating to the management and board, who are generally more interested in going forwards than "digging in the past". At the same time, a professional investigation may need time to be conclusive. To balance these aspects of a professional investigation, you may need to engage external specialists, such as those with forensic or accounting skills. As always, it may be expensive, but to undermine or compromise the investigation may be even more expensive.

Not all reports that come in through whistle-blowing or reports to managers are cases of suspected fraud, corruption, money laundering, theft or similar wrongdoing. These types of allegations normally represent a minor part of the incoming cases. Incoming cases can be allegations of discrimination, harassment, retaliation, privacy breeches, suspect interaction with a competitor, security concerns, health and safety matters or other labour-related matters. To ensure consistency in the handling and reporting of all cases, we recommend one point of receipt and administration of incoming cases, the Special Investigations office. The Special Investigations office then normally hands over matters that may more reasonably be investigated by other departments in the company, such as HR, Internal Audit or Security who report back to Special Investigations after concluding the investigation. However, these other departments may not have the relevant competence or resources to carry out professional investigations, so depending on the allegations and certainly if there is a pattern of claims of discrimination, harassment or retaliation, which are all signs of weak ethics and compliance culture in the management, special investigations or external competent resources should manage the investigations. As we can see from the case relating to Uber, this was a hard lesson for the management and the Board of Directors at Uber.

Investigations should be adequately overseen by the CECO and executive management. We have worked with various organisational set-ups but one example which has proven to be effective is an executive ethics committee (see page 76 above), held, as a suggestion, in conjunction with each executive management meeting. Each month new cases, updates, remediation and disciplinary procedures are discussed in this management forum. This practice enforces a strong commitment and transparency as well as awareness of "what is actually" happening in the organisations. Violations of the Code of Conduct and internal investigations should also be reported to the Board of Directors or one of its subcommittees. An important lesson here is that the committees need to ensure that they have a transparent and comprehensive overview of all cases coming in. From a board perspective, it is important that it is clear to them what cases are included in the report and presented to them and whether some cases are excluded from the statistics. Perhaps they are excluded because they have not been reported through the whistle-blowing channel but directly to management, or perhaps because the investigations are not carried out by Sspecial Investigations but somewhere else. We have seen horrific examples where the board actually only saw a fraction of the cases coming in due to the fact that these cases were handled "directly" by mid-management. This may give a false sense of comfort.

Denial

It is very human to react with denial, frustration, anger, white-washing and appeasement when the company, you or someone in your team is accused of wrongdoing. Especially when the accuser is someone, "who does not even dare to speak up in the open" but hides behind whistle-blowing channels and the ethics and compliance team. Many times, we have found that managers and executives are more interested in finding out who has blown the whistle than anything else in the investigation that may follow, upon a whistle-blowing. We all need to fight the urge to run to the trenches and defend ourselves. Managers need to fight their natural instinct to manage and let the investigation run its course.

You can learn a lot from your mistakes when you are not busy denying them.

Denial – we have done nothing illegal, this is a top-performer who has been in the company for 15 years that you are accusing, excuses (these are rumours spread by people who wish us ill), victimisation and anger (the journalists are idiots, have their own agenda and hunt in packs, we should sue them, alternatively, the investigation is full of holes, tendentious, and the ethics and compliance people are paranoid) are human reactions to information that one perceives as assault. We react very similarly when we are under attack, and it is the reptile brain talking. Very rarely is anger and denial the right path forwards – maybe the company is actually totally innocent, the journalists are idiots or investigator a real amateur and denial is truly right…but not as a first resort, only after careful considerations. However, most often the best approach is to get the denial and anger out of the system quickly and be open to the fact that wrongdoing happens all the time in any company.

To do a whole poodle – a Swedish idiom that means to admit unconditionally that you have done wrong and you prostrate yourself for forgiveness, putting on an act of remorse and self-reproach. It is indeed an act, a circus trick conceived by communications experts and not the same thing as real recognition of wrongdoing. A poodle will not cut to the core of the problem and will not support an effective ethics and compliance programme.

Without true acknowledgement of wrongdoing, there can never be proper remediation and without remediation, your compliance programme will never be effective. The whole programme will be built on a poor foundation without recognition of wrongdoing and guilt. Not only by the ethics and compliance team but also by the management and board. If you're ever in dialogue with authorities on corporate misconduct and subsequent remediation, public acknowledgement of guilt will be a central element.

Red flags, the duck test and inferences

One of the biggest frustrations when conducting internal investigations is when you have a certainty of there being truth to the allegations, but you are not able to prove it. In order for management to act, you must bring enough hard facts and proof to the table. It is of utmost importance that the investigations are handled with the highest sense of integrity, and we acknowledge that there may be malicious claims or claims simply without merit.

Nevertheless, at some point in the investigations, an experienced ethics and compliance officer or investigator "knows" that, more likely than not, there is truth to the claims. It is very important to not jump to conclusions and discipline people where there is not enough evidence of wrongdoing. It is also very important to not let wrongdoing pass without remediation. Where do we draw the line for wrongdoing that requires remediation or disciplinary action? How much proof is required? Proof of what – overstepping the internal rules, unethical behaviour or illegal behaviour? If you are not willing to discipline and remediate when overstepping "only" the internal rules and require proof of illegal behaviour as if in a criminal court and not a corporate environment, then the internal rules are redundant and should be changed to reflect this legalistic approach. The ethics committee must learn to look at red flags and inferences, to see what patterns they provide and understand when they look at a conclusion that will only be more substantiated with additional investigative resources and time. From the perspective of the CECO it is important to document the rationale for why certain "unresolved" investigations have been closed as well as the conclusions relating to remedial and disciplinary actions.

Red flags

A red flag is information that indicates that something may be wrong. A red flag is not in itself proof of, for example, bribery or fraud; it is just information that one needs to look further to see if the red flag has an acceptable explanation and can be "lowered" or if with further information that comes up the red flag becomes a certainty or additional red flags appear. As an example, it is a red flag if the company acting as an agent is registered in an offshore country with weak governance and low taxes. Further information is required. It is an additional red flag if it is impossible to establish the ultimate beneficial owner, the "UBO" of the agent. Further information is required. An additional red flag – a big one – is that the agent's contract stipulates payments to the agent as a percentage of deals made. After additional investigations, it becomes clear that payments to the agent amount to millions of dollars due to successful closure of a very big contract, but the effort of the agent seems to be limited to "opening doors", another very big red flag. The investigation has not been able to lower any of the red flags but also has not found evidence of how the agent has spent the millions easily earned by securing the contract "opening doors". The inferences you can make of the red flags in this case is that the likelihood of bribery is very high and depending on which legislation is applicable to the situation, there is a high legal risk. Regardless of jurisdictional reach, the conduct also presents a substantive ethical expectations risk as well as a high reputational risk.

The investigation may not be as clear and conclusive as you may wish. It may leave doubt. Maybe there isn't all the evidence you need to prove criminal acts such as fraud or bribery but you have many red flags, such as process deviations, unclear documentation for procurement decisions, technical acceptance and goods received. Invisible or unclear UBOs in the involved legal entities, a lot of adverse information ("smoke") but no hard evidence of politically exposed persons, PEPs, different conflicting statements, etc. Red flags that give you a pattern but not the famous smoking gun. What do you do? The internal investigations department is not the prosecutor and does not have access to the same resources as the police and prosecutor. The ethics committee is also not a criminal court, where the prosecutor has full burden of proof. The committees can and must look at the investigation and conclusions with a view to building a corporate culture of ethics and compliance, a culture of doing the right thing. Unfortunately, ethics and compliance officers do not have the silver bullet for these situations but can only offer advice based on experience. In evaluating the suspicious conduct and the consequences of this conduct, leaders may have to rely on the experience of those who regularly handle cases like this (the famous "gut") and evaluate the "red flags" to see if they show a pattern that indicates a crime or otherwise unacceptable behaviour. One needs to be aware of how the reptile brain reacts and might have to accept that while illegal conduct can only be established by the police and prosecutor, the company can elaborate with concepts of trust, distrust and requirements of ethical business conduct.

The Duck Test – if it looks like a duck, swims like a duck and quacks like a duck, it probably is a duck.

We like to draw a picture to visualise how inferences may be drawn with enough clear red flags, bringing us back to when we were kids and drew pictures by connecting numeric dots that seemed incomprehensible at first but when connected with a visible line became a picture of a house, a doll or a dog. Or a duck. The dots are the red flags, and the lines and the duck that emerge are the inferences you can draw from the investigation carried out. If it looks like a duck, swims like a duck and quacks like a duck, then it probably is a duck. If the red flags of the case look and smell like fraud, then you can probably infer that it is fraud.

To see a duck from only one dot is hard, but when you have a certain number, you will see the

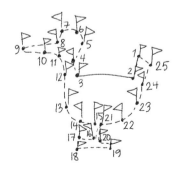

duck. To infer fraud from one red flag makes a shaky case, but with a certain number and quality of the red flags, you will see the fraud scheme.

Inferences – dare to know

In general, a fraud or corruption scheme is conceived
by intelligent and conniv-
ing criminals. Otherwise,
it fails early on. The scheme
normally includes elaborate
mechanisms to conceal and

cover the tracks. The aim is to not leave supporting documentation and a trail for the investigator to follow. You have to dare to know even if you do not have 100 % of the evidence. You have to stand up for what you believe – that something is wrong even if someone may never be proven guilty in a criminal court.

Human Rights Grievance Mechanism

A human rights grievance mechanism is a complaint process that can be used by individuals, workers, communities and/or civil society organisations that are being negatively affected by certain business activities and operations. It may be a good idea to seek technical and operational opportunities to open the whistle-blow-ing path also for human rights grievances. These cases will however require different protocols and competence for investigations. A human rights grievance mechanism also requires the company to be prepared to investigate and remediate the grievance.

Speak Up and Investigations – a quick checklist

- ✓ The whistle-blowing path should be easy to find and use and available to both employees and external parties.

- ✓ Protect the anonymity and confidentiality of the whistle-blower throughout your investigation process and afterwards.

- ✓ Establish a policy for non-retaliation and ensure that cases of retaliation are investigated. Train your HR organisation in identifying and managing cases of retaliation.

- ✓ Note that people may have different motives for reporting. Even with not so noble motives, such as greed and revenge, the case itself can have merits.

- ✓ Speaking truth to power is difficult and uncomfortable facts can easily be filtered out on its way upwards in the organisation.

- ✓ It is human to "run to the trenches" and defend the company and accused employees. Oftentimes it is not so productive.

- ✓ Investigation is a different discipline from Internal Audit and should preferably belong to the ethics and compliance organisation.

- ✓ Internal Special Investigations do not have access to the same investigative tools as the police or prosecutors have. It is important to not jump to conclusions but equally important to understand inferences and red flags.

- ✓ A special investigation should also aim to establish the core problem.

- ✓ Whistleblowing and investigations should be reported to management and to the board.

Remediation, disciplinary and corrective actions

Remediation is a fancier word for understanding what went wrong and fixing the problem. After an internal investigation, the investigative team may conclude that something has gone seriously wrong. Maybe the act in question is illegal, maybe it is unethical, maybe it is against your policies and procedures or maybe the company have simply lost trust in the wrongdoer – a whole scale of different but yet similar conclusions. It is possible that it is impossible to, with the means you have available for internal investigations, prove that a payment made is a bribe. You may have to conclude that the payment is inexplicable, illogical or contrary to internal policies and procedures or otherwise "fishy". The management committee, the ethics committee of the company may even have decided to let the wrongdoer go as a measure of disciplinary action. Also in this case, it is highly likely that the instinct is to close the case and move on. Who wants to rub salt in the wound? However, you cannot follow the money unless you involve the authorities. The police and prosecutors have access to better investigative tools and resources, so what is only a suspicion today may be corroborated by new proof further down the line. When a crime can reasonably be suspected, it is best to be proactive and self-report to the police or relevant authority. Sitting back and hoping for the best is not a great strategy and seldom works out for the company. You may even ask yourself if it is not the company that is a victim of a possible crime; therefore, you have duty towards the stakeholders of the company to report the suspected crime. It may come at a price of high fines and public disgrace if the suspicion turns out to be correct and there is a crime committed, for which the company is held responsible. However, the price for not being transparent and proactive may be much higher in lost trust and credibility when investigative journalists, whistle-blowers or other unforeseen events let the cat out of the bag. Some authorities, such as DOJ and SFO, will punish corruption harshly but encourage self-reporting through credits against the fines; this should certainly be an incentive as any credit against the high fines is beneficial for the company. However, in the end, you should self-report a suspected crime because it is the right thing to do.

Disciplinary actions

Remedial actions, consequences, as well as corrective and disciplinary actions, are important factors for an effective compliance programme. Ethics subcommittees of the board, management ethics committees, an ethics and compliance team, a fancy Code of Conduct, a great speaking-up line and special investigations come to naught if there are no consequences for failures, illegal, unethical or unwanted behaviour. Neither the ethics and compliance team nor the special investigations unit decide on consequences, this is part of the duties of the relevant management committee. Disciplinary actions can, for example, be oral warnings, formal written warnings and dismissal, possible demotion or change of responsibilities. You will also increasingly see companies claim back bonuses, as demonstrated in the case of Barclays CEO (page 104 above). In March 2017, Rolls Royce announced[25] that "in cases where employees have been dismissed or resigned as a result of Rolls-Royce's own internal investigation, shares and incentives have been cancelled in full as a consequence of the termination of their employment".

The management might also see it as fitting to require additional compulsory training or similar to encourage behavioural change. It is important to have fair, consistent and relevant disciplinary actions throughout the organisation. It is not ok if the same offence gets an oral warning when the offender works at a high level in the

---

25 http://www.telegraph.co.uk/business/2017/03/09/rolls-royce-claws-back-pay-employees-linked-bribery-scandal/

company but dismissal when found at a lower level. It is unfortunate but not uncommon to get side tracked and consider the offender's good sides and contribution to the company over the years when discussing and deciding disciplinary actions. Perhaps an excellent sales manager has engaged in some unacceptable entertainment or sales promotional activities, and the management and ethics committee are reluctant to deal with disciplinary actions because of the good figures and results that this person delivers. The end does not justify the means, and good people do bad things, maybe because they feel pressured to deliver results, but there has to be consequences of wrongdoing and breaches of internal rules or the law. Fair, transparent and consistent consequences – actions (consequences) or not taking action (no consequences) – send a clear message to the organisation. In the case of the sales manager above, maybe the ethics committee, in addition to disciplinary actions, should consider evaluating the incentive system for sales or general entertainment practices as a root cause of wrongdoing in the sales process. Regardless of how the case is handled, it sends a clear message to the rest of the organisation as to whether management actually care about how things are done when push comes to shove or not. It also sends a message about whether one should speak up and raise concerns – because if there are no consequences, why should one speak up?

It is also not ok if the practice of disciplinary actions varies from country to country, which brings us to different local legal restrictions to use disciplinary actions in consequence management. In some countries, there are stronger labour laws and strong unions protecting employees, also in cases of wrongdoing. Our experience tells us that this argument is sometimes used as an excuse to not discipline the offender and can be disregarded. On the other hand, sometimes the law and the unions provide a real challenge in executing disciplinary actions. The need to demonstrate resolve in acting on wrongdoing and being fair and consistent is so pivotally important; thus, it is worth putting up a fight against the laws and unions in each specific case. At the end, and worst case scenario, the company may have to "buy" the offender out from the company. AA solution that seems rather unfair for the company but is still better than giving in and doing nothing.

Too close for comfort

When I was less experienced, in my capacity as CECO, I sometimes agreed to be the "bearer of bad news" and undertook the very uncomfortable task of sitting down with the offender to deliver the bad news of oral or formal warnings or even dismissals. I rarely, if ever, agree to this anymore. It is the task of the manager together with HR to manage the employees and stand up for the rules and values of the company. It is equally important that the reason for the disciplinary action is made clear and the deliberations of the ethics committee communicated and understood. Sometimes, it may be tempting to blame the "compliance people" to ease up the tension in the room, but that is not very productive for the purpose of building a culture of compliance and ethics throughout the company. The ethics and compliance department does not build the culture, the managers and leaders do.

I have been in a situation where the offender was a member of my legal and compliance team, and it was no small offence either but a situation of accepting bribes. It goes to show there are no safe zones in the company, and I was just as surprised, shocked and offended, as any manager would have been, when this surfaced under my watch. Then it was I, who had to step aside and let the investigation run its course without my involvement or interference. My task, as the manager of the offender, was to handle the very difficult meeting to deliver the results of the investigation, deliberations of the ethics committee and the dismissal. A humbling experience that gives perspective on "being on the other side" of the investigation and a very personal experience of how good people can do bad things. I can also be perfectly honest and let you know that I had felt that "something was wrong" for quite a while before the whistle-blow came that initiated the investigation, but I had not acted upon this "gut" feeling, except with finding silly explanations and excuses for very odd behaviour. I hope that next time I will find the courage to act when I suspect something seems "not right". It might save time, money and personal suffering.

We are not flippant and insensitive; we believe that people should be treated with empathy and respect. However, if there are no consequences for the wrongdoing, how can you expect people to respect the common rules and how do you then build a culture of ethics, compliance and integrity? Your instinct may tell you to talk and report as little as possible about the concluded cases, especially the cases that lead to disciplinary actions; however, from an effective compliance perspective, it is the opposite. We strongly advocate being transparent in your reporting also on whistle-blowing, investigations, remediation and disciplinary actions, but we are not in favour of bringing the pillory back from its well-deserved grave. It may be a deterrent to read about other people's failures, shame and misery, but in our view to name and shame individuals also sends out signals of reigning by fear, and fear is not how you promote a culture of transparency and integrity. It is important that people understand that the company takes business ethics and compliance seriously and that there are consequences for wrongdoing, so reporting on whistle-blowing cases, investigations, disciplinary and other actions is important to show resolve and determination. Make it visible that it is not okay to violate the common rules and expectations of behaviour. Even if we promote transparency of "the dark side of human behaviour", this must be done with the highest respect towards privacy and individuals.

Acknowledgment of wrongdoing is the necessary baseline.

Acknowledgment of wrongdoing is the necessary baseline for remediation, disciplinary and corrective actions. Without acknowledgement of wrongdoing, there will be little heart and meaning of remediation; rather, it will be a side-activity, driven, in large part, by the ethics and compliance team. We come back to this again and again, but it is surprising how often important directors and managers do not fully buy in to the general messages of wrongdoing and mea culpa. They may play the game for a while, when things are urgent and new, but they do not believe in change; they become obstacles for transformation and they contribute negatively in the friction that the ethics and compliance programme produces. With enough of this resistance, the ethics and compliance people risk breaking from pressure and friction, and the programme risks becoming a tick-in-the-box exercise. If the company is in real trouble, has violated laws and is negotiating for an agreement with the prosecutor, the acknowledgement of wrongdoing will include acknowledgement of having committed a crime – an acknowledgement often proceeded by very difficult discussions with a lot of friction – believe us!

The blame game - the rogue employee

Instead of taking a serious look at the internal culture(s), policies, processes, governance, measurements and leadership, it is tempting to blame a situation that has gone all wrong in a company on the famous "rogue employee". One, two or maybe a group of employees who have acted in their own interest, have gone crazy, are criminals or have not understood their limitations are to blame. So the "bad guys" are replaced with new people and all is well. This is because you want to believe that the company is, at the core, a good company and the new people are good people, so all will be well again. It is the right thing to do, to change people. Preferably sooner rather than later, and make sure to change the right people at the right levels. After each crisis or major compliance breakdown that we have experienced, our conclusion has been that the company did not let go of enough people. If the intention is to change the culture, leadership and approach to business ethics and compliance, some token pawns will not suffice. The resistance from leaders and employees who are still working under the old assumptions and messages might prove overwhelming, and no real transformation will take place. However, as important as it is to replace the wrongdoers with new people, this does not transform the company, in fact, very little changes – it is after the change of people that the hard work to actually change the company can begin.

Remediation, disciplinary and corrective actions – a quick checklist

✓ Ensure that you create a list for remedial action and follow-up at the executive/board level.

✓ Without acknowledgement of wrongdoing, remediation will fail.

✓ The most important but also most challenging part of the ethics and compliance work is to ensure that individuals are held accountable.

✓ Create a methodology for disciplinary action and ensure that the measures are implemented.

✓ Establish and correct root causes of conduct failures, replacing people may only be the start of a long journey towards improved culture.

✓ If questioned by the authorities, they will ask for a list of individuals who were involved and ask what kind of disciplinary measures have been taken.

✓ Understand that fixing the problems (remediation) and disciplining individuals is very challenging and will cause friction and dilemmas – top management must take responsibility for execution.

✓ Systematically monitor remedial and disciplinary actions – and escalate to the board if needed – they have the right to know how discipline is ensured and that the same misconduct is not being repeated.

Third parties

Third parties … it is definitely possible to write an entire book about this part of the programme. In this book, we will keep it to a more reasonable level, even though it is a big topic and the most challenging part of the compliance programme.

The anti-bribery and corruption as well money laundering legislation in many countries are clear that payments made through third parties are also considered bribes, for which you are responsible. According to US enforcement statistics, more than 90 % of corruption cases involve intermediaries.[26] Payments can be labelled as, for example, charitable contributions, sponsorships, donations, consulting fees, business advisors, logistics brokers or technical fees. The specification in the agreement does not matter; it is what the third party actually does that counts. Funds, ultimately intended as bribes, may also be hidden in payments to vendors where the deliverables are unclear or the invoice inflated, or hidden in expense or travel expense claims. Similarly, a distributor may pay exorbitant prices to enable the creation of a slush fund for bribes. The days when employees travelled to foreign countries with bags of cash in order to pay bribes or grease the wheels are over; today, bribe givers and bribe takers are cleverer than that. In many cases, the scenarios are structured with agreements skilfully crafted by lawyers and legal opinions, comforting many seasoned business executives that the legal risk can be avoided. This strategy may have worked previously but is no longer very successful, as we see from recent corruption cases. In the Rolls Royce case, the company paid 671 MGBP in criminal penalties in a settlement with the UK, for claims of bribery through intermediaries. In the VimpelCom case (Veon), the company settled with the US and

---

26   EYs 12th Global Fraud Survey found that 90 per cent of reported FCPA cases involved allegations about actions taken by third parties. Third parties that have been the focus of FCPA enforcement include customs brokers, freight forwarders, distributors, sales agents, consultants and joint venture partners.

the Netherlands, for 795 MUSD, for bribes paid through entering into a joint venture agreement with a local partner in Uzbekistan. It did not help that the Board of Directors for VimpelCom had two legal opinions provided by law firms for their ease of mind that the transaction was not a violation of US corruption law. In the Telia Company case, the company agreed to pay 965 MUSD in criminal penalties to the US and the Netherlands, for a similar joint venture structure in Uzbekistan. In the statement of facts of the settlement agreement, we can read about lawyers advising the management to structure the deal so that US jurisdiction was avoided. This legal advice was not helpful for Telia in the end.

"If one carries out business in a corrupt country, one should quite simply be more thorough than TeliaSonera has been. ... If one doesn't know who a counterparty is, nor how a counterparty has obtained the assets being acquired, it would seem difficult to ensure that corruption has not occurred at some step along the way".

MSA press release 1 February 2013

This was [part of] the conclusion by the Mannheimer Swartling (MSA) law firm that carried out an investigation in Telia Company (at the time TeliaSonera) into the, at the time alleged, bribery in Uzbekistan.

Third parties cause a lot of headaches in other conduct risk areas as well. The BP oil rig was operated by a subcontractor, the factory in Rana Plaza was operated by subcontractors, and the child labour in the Stora Enso supply chain was in a subsidiary (with less than 20 % ownership by Stora Enso). Poor working

Not knowing is not the answer anymore

conditions, issues with health and safety and slave labour are all issues that mainly arise out of the supply chain. There are privacy concerns in large outsourcing contracts to countries where security and privacy are not high on the agenda and labour is cheap[-er]. From a strictly contractual point of view, it may be possible to limit the legal exposure but not so when it comes to responsibility for human rights, meeting ethical expectations or reputational damage.

The concept of third parties is wide; employees are third parties before they are employed. The same goes for board members. Suppliers, consultants, agents, distributors, business partners, joint venture partners and companies on the acquisition list are all third parties. Banks, financiers, brokers, lawyers and auditors are third parties too and also part of your operations and responsibility. Simply put, you need to know who you are doing business with, who you are paying, why and for what. Some companies are more advanced than others, when it comes to assessing, managing and controlling their supply and value chain. Typically, these are companies manufacturing products with high levels of quality and security requirements, such as the car industry. The same may go for companies in the fashion/garment industry, where public opinion, media and scandals have prompted action from the company to understand who is actually making their clothes and under what conditions. Other companies are less aware of their third party risk. They may have outsourced a large part of their core business without any thought of responsibility for work conditions, privacy or other human rights, focusing on demands for cost savings or maintained high margins. Some companies have decentralised procurement processes, which make it very challenging to control whether a local customs broker is used to "speeding up the process". In some countries, it is "impossible" to do business without the use of a local agent, who gets a percentage of the contract value but does not really contribute to the business with any tangible deliverables. In some industries, it is just plain industry practice to use a third party's unreasonably expensive fees, judging from the efforts and work performed, to "broker" big contracts with states and governments. In some countries, it is not possible to find out who owns a business, as there are no registers, and just the effort to try to uncover an opaque owner is illegal. In some countries, the workers have no shoes, and a hardhat has never been heard of. The local equivalent of the US Occupational, Safety and Health Administration consists of employees with low pay, making the inevitable demand for a bribe to issue a permit, as the only way of supporting their growing family. In some countries, there is a tradition to "import" work force for seasonal or hard labour tasks and pay them such low salaries that the term slavery comes to mind.

The bottom line is – you need to look into who is part of your supply and value chain, who you do business with and who represents the firm.

Regardless of the circumstances, the bottom line is – you need to look into who is part of your supply and value chain, who you do business with and who represents the firm. Do not forget mergers, acquisitions and divestments – there are several big cases involving bribery in mergers and acquisitions – you have to know who you are buying from or selling to, how the transaction and payment flows are structured, and whether there is a local partner/middleman involved. In addition, you have to understand whether there are any legacy risks coming from the acquired target. Our experience is that when you acquire a private company in a high-risk jurisdiction, it is very likely that they have a completely different view on bribes and facilitation payments. During the acquisition phase, you are not likely to uncover these kinds of set ups and you have to move in with your third party programme as soon as possible to ensure whether there are some payments that you have to stop immediately – and under some circumstances, report to the authorities.[27]

There are also third party risks in terms of employees, as employees are third parties before they become employees. We have encountered several circumstances where the company, at least in the head office, are unaware of daughters, nephews and brothers of government officials working at the subsidiaries. Commonly, these individuals have gotten their jobs outside of the ordinary recruitment process and probably as response to a request or as a favour, a bribe. The JPMorgan case[28] involved giving internships to the children of Chinese officials – "princelings". So, ensure that you have fair and unbiased hiring processes globally. Do the background checks. Some industries are somewhat "incestuous" and hire from each other; one person can spend his or her entire professional career in the same industry. This may be a great thing, ensuring solid competence in the core business, but it also enables unwanted behaviour to spread, developing an industry culture.

It is also vital to know who sits on the boards, especially in subsidiary and joint venture boards. In many countries, especially emerging markets, the line between the public and private sector is blurred. You want to know whether you have the trusted advisor of the prime minister sitting in your board.

---

27 The concept of successor liability under US FCPA involves self-reporting to the authorities to avoid being liable for the misconduct going forward. See DOJ opinion release for more information https://www.justice.gov/sites/default/files/criminal-fraud/legacy/2014/11/14/14-02.pdf

28 https://www.justice.gov/opa/pr/jpmorgan-s-investment-bank-hong-kong-agrees-pay-72-million-penalty-corrupt-hiring-scheme

Third Party management - a risk-based process

There are many ways to structure the work. The main elements of a third party management process can be structured as follows:

- Checking business rationale and confirming internal "owner" of third party relationship
- Unbiased and objective selection process, including screening of related individuals and Ultimate Beneficial Owners, "UBO" and potential involvement of Politically Exposed Persons "PEP"
- Contracting, including ABC provisions and audit rights
- Training and advising on your framework of rules, the Supplier / Business Partner Code of Conduct
- Managing and monitoring the relationship, for example, work reports on actual work done/deliverables, on-site audits and understanding changes in ownership
- Reacting and improving, how do we treat misconduct or non-compliance
- Governance structure and escalation processes

Each element requires time, effort and relevant competence; thus, it is easy to understand that in a company with a decentralised view on third party management, it will be more challenging to implement, requiring more resources, escalation processes and coordination. From a cost perspective, it may make sense to invest in a global function that can do the screening work and identify risks from databases such as ownership records, assessment of sustainability reports and performance as well as financial records. The most important thing is to ensure that each element of the third party process is systematically implemented and documented – again what is not documented is not done.

There will always be discussions as to whether it is necessary to include all third parties in the process. Do we have to document the business rationale and do screening for every single one? If you ask the regulators, the answer is you need to demonstrate that you have a risk-based approach. And the risk-based approach cannot be random; it should be systematic and consistent. You will have to develop a methodology for assessing who your third parties are, what they do for you and where the biggest risks are. To put a process in place, based on the elements described going forwards, for new suppliers or sales agents, is one thing; it is hard work and taxing on everybody's patience. To put the processes in place for your existing stock of suppliers, agents, partners and charities, the "backlog" is even more challenging and requires determination and support from the very top. Any "backlog" project is also a cross-functional effort, involving all functions that have links to third parties or payments to third parties. This is where the compliance programme is either successful or a failure. This is where the substantial friction and dilemmas must be solved, with the support of escalation processes and relevant management level attention. In practice, we know that this is very difficult and takes time to achieve, but it is important to see and acknowledge the difference between what is required from us and what is possible to achieve today and over time.

The risk of corruption, money laundering and fraud may be smaller if the vendor is a company providing cleaning services than if it is a company providing consultant or sales promotion services or other third parties, where it is more difficult to understand what the third party actually supplies. Even if we require a supplier to sign a Supplier / Business Partner Code of Conduct, we cannot assume that that will fix the supplier conduct risk. Also, a third

It is important to see and acknowledge the difference between what is required from us and what is possible to achieve today and over time.

party needs to have a process in place, ensuring that the words in the Supplier / Business Partner Code of Conduct are put into action. But how do you decide when a deviation is too much and when it is acceptable? In one company, we have seen a "compliance compass" that was developed for this purpose. The compass includes the requirements from the Supplier / Business Partner Code of Conduct and then lists possible deviations per content area. The compass also provides guidance as to when and to whom escalation of a decision is required.

Third party compliance compass

More often than not, you have third parties who are not capable of complying with your rules. It is not for lack of understanding your rules but can instead be a consequence of the chal-  lenging external context or different stage of maturity than your own company. You have to decide when non-compliance with a specific conduct risk, for example, labour practices as described in the Supplier / Business Partner Code of Conduct, is a reason for terminating the relationship or when a development plan is more appropriate. The guidance is there to ensure consistency and escalation routes if needed.

Example
Anti-Corruption – Transparency in ownership structure

Introduction	Regulation	Risk	Guidelines	Mitigate/ avoid
We need to know who we are doing business with in order to ensure that we are not complicit in illicit activity. Knowing the UBO enables monitoring and managing risk for corruption and conflict of interests and sanctions violations.	UK Bribery Act, FCPA, the European Union Anti-Money Laundering and Terrorist Financing Directive and sanctions laws as well as Supplier / Business Partner Code of Conduct.	Legal, ethical and societal risks relating to bribery and corruption, terrorist financing, fraud, money laundering and sanctions. Such dealings could damage reputation, undermine customer confidence and cause a strong political reaction.	– Request identification and company documents from the third party. (1) what corporate structure is used (2) who are the shareholders and what is the shareholding (3) who are the UBOs (if any) (4) was the company recently set up (5) is the third party incorporated in a tax haven (6) is the third party fully or partially state-owned and (7) is the third party directly involved in the business for which it is being retained – Check the obtained information against central/national registries	– Undisclosed information about ownership – inconsistencies/gaps in information – anti-corruption contract clause – ensure a high level of transparency in the tender and payments

△ Minor issue	△ Major issue	△ Critical finding
The ownership structure and the UBOs are disclosed with minor inconsistencies – no reason to suspect deliberate lack of transparency.	Limited transparency about ownership structure, and there are some concerns about deliberate lack of transparency.	Ownership structure and the UBOs are not disclosed, and there is reason to suspect deliberate lack of transparency.

Example
Human Rights – general

Introduction	Regulation	Risk	Guidelines	Mitigate/avoid
The third party should engage proactively in order to improve over time, with the aim to meet high standards of human rights, both in the workplace and more broadly, within its sphere of influence.	UN Declaration of Human Rights, UN Global Compact, UK Modern Slavery Act, Supplier / Business Partner Code of Conduct	Human rights risk, reputational risk, legal and ethical risk	The Code of Conduct requires that third parties have in place a policy on human rights, which includes treating all employees (including those employed by subcontractors) with dignity and respect. All employees working directly or indirectly for the third party shall be aware of these basic rights. This includes access to basic amenities (such as drinking water and toilets) and that employees shall have the possibility to raise concerns without fear of punishment or retribution.	A corrective action plan could include: (1) increasing worker and management awareness of fundamental human rights, (2) establishing a human rights policy and (3) introducing management systems to avoid and/or mitigate the risk of human rights violations.

△ Minor issue	△ Major issue	△ Critical finding
The third party has no formal policy on human rights and/or there is no formal channel for raising concerns or grievances.	There are indications of human rights violations but appear to be non-systematic or non-material.	The third party shows little or no regard for human rights and/or there is evidence of systematic violations or violations other than non-material.

Exceptions - deviations - plan

A minor, a major or sometimes even a critical issue may not be a showstopper for engaging the third party. Guidance for the decisions should be defined, as the compass shows above, in for example the instructions and guidelines for procurement, sales and marketing, sponsorships and donations as well as your ABC instructions. The different escalation processes will define governance for decisions, and the different corporate committees or persons responsible will develop practices. Having consistent practices transparently communicated internally to the employees who work with the due diligence and the compass evaluation of third parties will support them in future considerations and deliberations of third parties. Some critical or major findings may be showstoppers, while others are not. A third party who refuses to disclose the Ultimate Beneficial Owner (UBO), or third party with a UBO who is a Politically Exposed Person (PEP), in combination with uncertainties in how the assets of the company have been acquired or a vendor who is using child or slave labour are probably showstoppers for all business dealings. In some countries, you have local vendors that have never seen hard hats, steel-toe shoes (shoes may not be common at all, people use flip-flops) or harnesses. Your decision in such a case may be to make exceptions from your safety requirements and develop the vendor rather than using a global supplier who will probably use the local subcontractors anyway. Where the third party requires exemptions from the Supplier / Business Partner Code of Conduct, be it a minor, major or critical issue, there needs to be a plan for how and when the third party shall be up to an acceptable level. You also need dedicated resources to support the execution of the plan on your end, maybe with training or other activities, building the competence locally. Maybe you "only" require resources on your part to follow up on the plan, monitoring and auditing. With existing third parties, you may conclude that the findings are unacceptable and you need to exit the supplier. This may however be easier said than done; you may be contractually bound, there may be other dependencies or there may be a real lack of competitors to replace the third party. Instead of a development plan, you will need a plan on how to exit this third party, an exit-plan, which can withstand the scrutiny of challenges from stakeholders and authorities.

The third party process generates an abundance of friction in the company. This is normal, as there are so many conflicting interests and priorities but while normal, the friction can still be gruelling, destroy relations and wear people down. It is therefore important that the company develops clear policies, instructions and guidelines as well as processes, which include decision requirements and escalation processes to ensure that the decisions are made at the correct level of authority and responsibility and are consistent and transparently communicated.

Red Flags

We have discussed red flags in the context of investigations. A red flag is information that indicates that something may be wrong. As an example, there is information on the internet that the suggested vendor has problems with forced labour. This information is indeed a red flag and cannot be dismissed without further analysis. It may turn out that the information is false or that the supplier has addressed the problem and implemented a programme to come to terms with its issues in the work force. Subsequently, the red flag can be lowered. It is also a red flag when you have difficulties getting information from the third party. Maybe they refuse to fill out the written forms that you send them to request information. Another red flag is when you have an owner, a UBO, who seems illogical. How is it possible that this young man can own a company worth billions of dollars? Further research and information are required here. The red flag may have perfectly reasonable explanations, maybe it was an inheritance or maybe this is a young IT entrepreneur who made a fortune very early on; subsequently, the red flag can be lowered. It can also transpire that the young man has no business history, other than being the grandson of the president of the country. This is a big red flag, requiring more research and information and to be put into the larger context. Another red flag is if one distributor is having a substantially different pricing logic than other distributors. Can it be that a slush fund has been created, intending to pay bribes instead? One needs to evaluate all information and red flags and look at the whole picture to understand the risks involved with a third party. A red flag with a governmental official owning a company may be lowered if the contract and other circumstances, such as pricing logic, business justification and deliverables, make sense.

Human Intelligence in the third party process

The third party due diligence process may be compared to a cross-country running journey with many crossing paths, where you have to stop and think, assess and decide. Where you have to apply human intelligence and cannot only rely on automated reports. There are many excellent third party vendors, who provide supporting processes, tools and competence but, unless your business is very small, you need the core competence of third party management in-house. In a larger global business, you may need the competence locally, regionally and globally, depending on how the operations are structured.

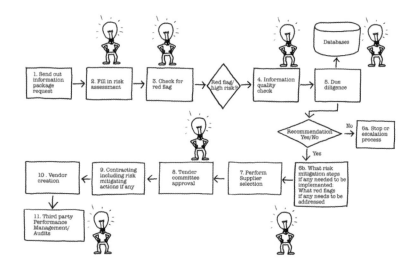

Do not get lost in the forest

As you probably understand by now, third party management is a cumbersome process. Ultimately, it is about asking, and assessing the answers to, a few simple questions – why, who, what and how.

Why do we need a third party and why this particular third party, *who* is the third party, *what* are they going to do, and *how* will we ensure that the third party is complying with our standards.

Why

The most critical question to understand is the why. In our experience, this is where most of the issues arise and can be resolved at an early stage, saving yourself and the company a lot of extra work and trouble. We have encountered numerous proposals for suppliers, agents and partners, where the *why* part has been very vague. Keep asking why until you truly understand that there is a commercially justifiable reason behind the third party relationship. If you do not get a clear response to the question why, if you cannot yourself justify the business relationship to the board and the outside world, do not approve and if needed, escalate, ultimately to the board. Answers to the *why* that will not suffice are, for example, "the customer requires this", "this is a local requirement, although not written in the law", "we cannot get the necessary licenses if we do not engage this third party". Answers to the why that *may* suffice include: "the advisor is an expert in our industry and knows the local regulation", "there may only be one tender every five years and we cannot afford to have our own sales people on the ground waiting for this one opportunity" and "the supplier is qualified to do the job and has resources to do it".

Who

This means you need to know who the physical owner of the legal entity that you do business with is. Sometimes, the owner is not the real owner but someone who is "fronting" for the real beneficial owner. Criminals are not idiots, so they will put children, wives, secretaries, old friends, and sometimes even complete strangers who are paid a small amount to be the goalkeeper. You need to know the real owner, the UBO. You also need to know if the UBO is a government official or politically exposed person or an owner that is a "red flag"; maybe, it is someone connected to employees or consultants inside the company and therefore a red flag for fraud. You need to know that the person is someone with whom you would want to be associated with and do business with. You need information that is reliable, evaluated and processed and that can form the basis of your knowledge of who you are doing business with. The due diligence/screening process that is required to understand who you do business with is complex; moreover, it requires skill and experience to understand the information about possible red flags that turn up in the process and to be able to sift through the material to evaluate the red flags and adverse information, enabling an enlightened decision at the end.

What

To understand the context, one needs to know what the contract pertains to, what is ordered, what is delivered and accepted. Do we have previous experience of the vendor? Is the contract commercially sound? Do deliverables and remuneration match? Can the supplier reasonably deliver under the contract? What is the sales agent going to do? What are their qualifications and do they have proven track record and expertise? A big red flag is when an agent or local partner is paid in percentage of the deal. It may seem very rational and sound business practice that an agent is "only" paid 5 % of the deal he or she can broker, but if the deal is big the amounts can become very big and totally out of sync in relation to the effort spent, creating plenty of room for bribes to be paid.

Poor controls and alignment between what you are paying for and what has been delivered and accepted leave room for creative fraud schemes as well as the establishment of "slush funds" to be used when paying bribes.

How

You will need to know how the work will be done and how you will monitor the work. How are the operations of the third party run? How are the working conditions at the supplier? Do the workers have shoes and hard hats or do they climb telephone poles without a harness? Is your supplier subcontracting work to less scrupulous vendors, who use forced or underage labour or dump waste in the river running past the factory? Have they agreed to your (or a similar) Supplier / Business Partner Code of Conduct? If so, are they living by it, or is it just lip service? Have you done site visits to check?

The business case for third party management

Let's be honest – an overhaul of the company's approach to third parties and implementing effective compliance that includes third parties is an exercise that requires spending money on people and processes. However, we are certain that this is not wasted money. We have found over and over again that by bringing in ethical business practices, compliance and controls on third parties, you actually save more money than you spend in the end. First, by challenging corrupt business practices, for example, the requests/extortion for "sponsorships and donations" commonly used by government officials in many countries, you may actually change the external behaviours and the requests will stop. You may also have been paying to agents for "nothing" and may well be able to do the sales with internal resources. Do not forget that the world is changing, and the governments in traditionally "corrupt" countries like China, Peru and Nigeria are at least to some extent trying to tackle corruption. Your customers are likely to be under the same requirements as you, and transparent and clean business is to their benefit as well. At the end of the day, bribes increase prices and eat up your margin. Second, fraud theory establishes that "opportunity" is an important requirement for fraud, and the lack of controls and responsible business approaches related to third parties mean many opportunities for money going out the door. We see fraud schemes repeatedly, involving subcontractors and "consultants", where employees have been stealing from the company. Such schemes are not minor; it is not uncommon that substantial amounts go undetected and have been paid to these fake "subcontractors" over the years. Thirdly, when you firm up your sales and procurement practices, you save money in general. Is there really a business case for several agents, dealers, distributors as well as having your own sales people in one country? How do you in this complex sales structure control quality and customer satisfaction? Objective selection criteria for purchases will mitigate the risk for buying from someone's cousins company at inflated prices. Fourthly, most corruption, fraud and bribery happen through third parties, and the consequences of high fines, lost trust and reputational damage as well as value deterioration are infinitely higher than any programme for effective compliance and controls for third parties. Finally, it is the right thing to do, as this is where a vast majority of violations against human rights, society and the environment happen.

Regardless of how the company organises the ownership of the conduct risks and compliance programmes, the responsibility relating to third parties is always going to be a very important part of any compliance programme. Somewhere in the organisation, therefore, you will need a team that is competent in conducting proper due diligence on third parties, not only for procurement and sourcing purposes but also for vetting partners, agents and distributors as well as supporting M&A activities. There are many great consultant companies providing these services, but regardless of how much of this work you will want to outsource, you will also need competence internally, not only for coordination and documentation purposes but also to increase competence and intelligence in the company itself. We have found it useful to set this team up as a shared service outside the Ethics & Compliance department to avoid the misperception that third parties which have gone through the due diligence process are "cleared" by Ethics & Compliance. It is our experience that you need highly qualified and experienced employees to do this work as it gives rise to difficult deliberations, dilemmas and causes a lot of friction.

Third parties – a quick checklist

- ✓ Why? Who? What? How?
- ✓ Manage third parties with a risk-based approach, keeping in mind that this is, by far, the biggest risk in the compliance programs.
- ✓ Have you done a risk assessment on your third parties?
- ✓ Do you know the nature and qualifications of your third parties?
- ✓ Have you implemented a risk-based due diligence process?
- ✓ Have you analysed the third parties that were contracted before the "new" due diligence process was implemented e.g. "the backlog"?
- ✓ Can you answer the question "How do you know that the company is not paying bribes as we speak?"?
- ✓ Make use of the audit and monitoring clauses in the contracts.

Reporting and Improvement

To use a model of ethics and compliance such as the one we suggest will ensure a well-designed programme. However, one needs to know if it is applied in good faith and if it is working. Otherwise, it will be like this  beautiful car without an engine; it will not take you anywhere. It might have served to blow smoke in the eyes of some prosecutors or regulators once upon a time, but not anymore, as they have become significantly savvier on ethics and compliance over the years. To understand whether the programme works, you need to have systematic follow-up and reporting of key deliverables and targets. You need to evaluate what works and not as part of continuously improving the programme, laying the foundations for planning the next steps and necessary revisions of the approach, scope and efforts. We also include reporting and engaging with external stakeholders in this cornerstone of ethics and compliance. In evaluating the context to understand which content (conduct risks) the ethics and compliance programmes should focus on, there is (or should be) a stakeholder dialogue. So, in a constructive dialogue, it is natural to report on not only the efforts and progress being made but also the struggles and dilemmas. By being transparent with your stakeholders, and involving them in your programme, you will not only be encouraged to improve but you will also invite a conversation about the difficulties and dilemmas and thus increase awareness and understanding that Rome was not built in a day.

Transparent reporting and external communication are natural parts of a well-implemented compliance programme. If you know what you are working with, how you are doing and how you should improve, you have nothing to hide. It is better that you take up your challenges with your stakeholders yourself than risk being exposed by the ever-increasing investigative media. You should engage in a dialogue with your stakeholders, so they understand the reality of where you operate. For shareholders, it is important to understand the true cost of their dividends. For NGOs and social interest groups, it is important to understand how the company is handling conduct risks and to align expectations on what can be achieved. If all global companies would be transparent about how challenging it is to ensure a sustainable and fair supply chain or how hard it is to avoid paying facilitation payments or other bribes in certain jurisdictions, it would be easier to tackle the core problem of corrupt governments, weak governance mechanisms, disrespect for human rights and eroding the environment. By engaging in a dialogue, the stakeholders, and especially shareholders, can put adequate requirements on the company and be engaged in creating long-term value for the company as well as for the external environment where the company is operating.

Try transparency and honesty

Especially in third party management, you often hear that it is "impossible" for a company to control its third party chain beyond the first tier of suppliers. It may seem impossible because the costs and work involved to achieve this control are overwhelmingly and maybe disproportionally high. We once heard an investor ask the question "how far does your responsibility reach in the supply chain?" to the head of sustainability of a global retail business. Her answer was "our responsibility goes all the way to the source, but we are not there yet. It is our aspiration but it takes time as there are many priorities to consider in the business". A good, honest and transparent answer which needs to be followed up with a good, honest and transparent account of what they are doing, what they have achieved thus far and what their plans are for achieving control throughout the value chain.

It is very tempting to avoid reporting or disclosing things that are not so good or are in a bad state. At the AGM in 2015, Telia Company held an open "pre-meeting" for sustainability reporting, with the possibility for questions and answers. We took the opportunity to talk about the challenges and difficulties we had encountered in implementing the anti-corruption programme, particularly in relation to third parties. The audience participants, who were also well versed in the area of responsible business and sustainability, gave very positive feedback, and many said it was a relief to hear some unvarnished truths. Especially in a situation where trust in the company is low, honesty and transparency are good medicine. The idea is not to blame previous management or anyone else, the purpose for the openness is to give intelligent people the opportunity to assess and evaluate the situation, actions and plans of the company. Transparency will give different stakeholders access to information and will take the burden off the management to work miracles.

Collective action - working together

Part of being transparent is working together with others. It may be hard to have a real impact on hostile, corrupt or indifferent governments or government officials alone, but the fact

"ALONE WE CAN DO SO LITTLE, TOGETHER WE CAN DO SO MUCH"

— HELEN KELLER

is that you are normally not alone. It is possible to work together with your competitors as well as stakeholders whom you normally do not engage with that often, such as the general public. The whole industry may have the same problems with certain behavioural risks, such as telecom operators that must acquire licenses and frequencies from governments, corrupt or not, to operate in a market. In 2016, a telecom industry integrity initiative was formed to discuss and evaluate what collaborative and collective actions may be available. The fashion industry which more or less all use suppliers from countries where there are problems with environmental harm, labour rights and health and safety are collaborating to bring the supply chain up to a 21st century standard. Also, the Maritime Anti-Corruption Network has been established to promote integrity in the maritime industry. In some countries, all global businesses struggle with the same problems of kleptocracy, with random demands for payments disguised as sponsorships, donations, fees or taxes. Why not work together to find ways to refuse paying? Another form of collaboration is with forums and groups of ethics and compliance professionals who, under "Chatham rules", share experiences, difficulties and solutions. Stakeholder collaboration, collective action and industry dialogues are central elements of a successful compliance programme. The aim is to even the playing field and drive long-term change towards improving the rights of others and to improve society and the environment wherever you do business.

What gets measured gets done

Reporting both internally and externally on the structure of the programme(s) including its status and progress is important in establishing trust that you are handling the behavioural risks with adequate determination. It helps you to find measurements, KPIs or other meaningful indicators of progress that make sense and can be understood by broader audiences. It forces you to plan, prioritise and execute. Enforcement agencies, such as SFO in the UK, DOJ, OSHA and SEC in the US, and the new French anti-bribery agency will require information on both the design of the compliance programmes and measurements of its effectiveness. Our experience is that they will ask very specific questions. They will ask "do you have a whistle-blowing system that enables anonymous reporting in the local languages?" Hopefully, the answer is yes, and the follow-up questions may be "How many whistle-blowing cases have been investigated?" "How many investigations have ended up in disciplinary actions?" "How many oral warnings, formal warnings or dismissals?" "How many weeks, on average, are required for an investigation?" "Have you done an employee survey to understand a) if the employees know of the whistle-blowing channel?, b) if they are inclined to use it? and c) for those who answer no on b) why not? Be prepared to answer with data and not only with your best guess. They may say, "you claim to have tone from the top commitment, but how do you ensure that leaders have personal commitment? How do you a) measure and test leaders on commitment for ethical business practices and b) interview prospective leaders on competence and commitment of ethical business conduct?"

KPIs – examples of numeric indicators to follow the ethics and compliance programme

Risk assessments: How many countries or business units, out of all, have done the ABC risk assessments? In how many countries, out of all, have you done a country risk assessment? In terms of percentage of all countries that the company operates in? How many leadership groups by percentage (at the global, divisional, regional and local level) in the company have shared the risk assessments in an actual meeting?

Organisation: How many face-to-face meetings have the board or one of its committees had with the CECO during the year? Out of these, how many of these meetings have been without the CEO or other representatives of the executive management? How many face-to-face meetings have the CEO and the CECO had? How many in the E&C team are certified in compliance, fraud investigations or similar?

Policies and Procedures: How many of the policies, instructions and guidelines, out of all existing, have been updated this year? How often do you "push" instructions out to employees for attestation? How many employees, by percentage, have signed and certified compliance with the Code of Conduct or ABC policy? How many of the established root causes for a Code of Conduct violation are related to circumvention of internal procedures and out of those, how many have previously been reported as a weakness in an internal audit or control testing?

Training and Communication: What is the budget for E&C training? Is it on an upward trend or downward? How many employees have been trained in face-to-face workshops? In terms of percentage, how many of the management meetings included one hour of discussion on ethical dilemmas?

Speak Up and Investigation: How many cases pertain to alleged violations of the travel and business entertainment policies? How many cases per country/cases per business unit/division? To measure the length of an investigation is a good *internal team* metric, however it may not be so fruitful to report upwards in the organisation to avoid premature closure of investigations and a pressure to speed up complex cases.

Remediation, Disciplinary and Corrective actions: How many whistle-blowing cases have ended up in disciplinary actions? How many dismissals? Have any of the cases on alleged retaliation ended up in disciplinary actions? Percentage of employees leaving who are invited to exit interviews? Management remediation response in days (from investigation recommendation to closure of disciplinary action or process improvement)? In how many of the investigations has the root-cause been identified and corrected?

Third parties: How many, out of the total, third parties have undergone due diligence? How many third parties classified as high risk have we continued to do business with? How many third parties have we continued to do business with against the recommendation of the due diligence team? How many vendors have been disapproved of or terminated? Percentage of vendors visited for site audits?

Leadership: How much time has been dedicated to responsible business, ethics and compliance and conduct risk at executive leadership meetings (in % of total)? How many of the new leaders employed or promoted are interviewed or tested on ethical values? How many leaders have participated in training on business ethics and human behaviour, such as ethical blindness, normalisation or avoidance? And on diversity and inclusion?

Oversight, monitoring, governance: How many audits, out of the total, by internal audit have been dedicated to conduct risk? Integration of conduct risk aspects into company employee barometer (note that overly positive answers from high risk jurisdictions indicate a need for a surprise compliance visit and not that things are fine).

Incentives

It is also great if one can manage to find incentives for desirable conduct. On the contrary, many incentives and bonus structures serve to push wrong behaviour such as sales bonuses for closed deals and a strong focus on quarterly or year-end results. A strong personal financial incentive can be difficult to resist if ethical business conduct is not projected as a priority. Many companies have however chosen to also include ethical and responsible business practices in their yearly performance reviews. This is good practice, even if it may be hard to find the right performance indicators to avoid too many discretionary and random evaluations.

ISO 37001 Anti-Bribery management system

Not only is the methodology of effective compliance used by regulators throughout the world to coach or force corporations to implement compliance programmes for different conduct risks, the same compliance requirements and methodology are also the basis for the new ISO standard for anti-bribery management systems. The ISO 37001 ABC management system is widely discussed; with some are very positive and some negative views. The criticism is, as far as we can find, not related to the actual content of the ISO standard but rather to the fact that the ISO 37001 may paint a useless or even false picture of the company certified, as there are no measurements of leadership, conduct and culture. Regardless, the standard provides a good overview of what constitutes "adequate procedures".

Reporting and improvement – a quick checklist

✓ Is the programme working? – What gets measured gets done – find data!

✓ Do you have KPIs on the organisation and management tied to the ethics and compliance programmes?

✓ Is the incentive programme in any aspect tied to promoting and building a culture of ethics and compliance?

✓ Transparent reporting, both on challenges and failures is a good baseline for building trust.

✓ Can you find a "collective" to work with?

Oversight, monitoring and governance

Oversight

The board and the executive management are responsible for ensuring that there are adequate procedures in place to manage compliance risk, regardless of whether or not they have appointed a CECO to lead the job. As the public expectations on responsible, ethical and compliant businesses increase, we foresee that it will be hard to argue that any procedures implemented are adequate or effective if there are no dedicated and qualified resources to lead the work. Appointing a CECO, with adequate authority, remit and autonomy is a central element of the programme. We argue that the ethics and compliance programme will be more effective with less organisational filters between the ethics and compliance team and the board. Based on our experience, it is very difficult for a person without relevant qualifications (in ethics and compliance methodology as well as qualifications in specific conduct risks, for example ABC) to lead the ethics and compliance work and implement a program that will protect the company and its stakeholders. We recommend formalising the interaction between the CECO and the board and, for example, agreeing that ethics and compliance, including internal investigations, shall be a standing agenda item for a board committee such as the audit and risk committee. In addition, we recommend setting a standard agenda item for the full board once a year, or more frequently if the situation requires. The board should exercise an independent review of the company's compliance programme.

The CECO should have "access" to the board. Access through the regular reports to the full board or relevant board committee but also opportunities to discuss the programmes with a representative of the board or relevant board committee alone, for example, in a pre-meeting to the regular meeting. The possibility for some "alone time" with a board representative is, in a sense, to protect the integrity and position of the CECO, to bring up matters that would be difficult for the CECO to otherwise get past the executive management layer. It may also somewhat limit the "friction" that may be a by-product of not agreeing with the executive management or CEO. It allows time to problematize and raise issues of concern, instead of providing facile solutions to complex problems. Another aspect is to ensure that the board have access to information that might get lost on the way upwards in the organisation. It is not about bypassing the executive management or the CEO, nor is it to put operational responsibilities on the board members. A CECO who escalates and reports random difficulties and tribulations to the board is not doing the job. The reports to the board should be structured accounts of the programmes, remediation gaps, increasing risks and escalation problems. We do not want to "put the monkey on the shoulders of the board members" but rather let them know there is a monkey on the loose. Supporting the board to question the information they are fed, asking relevant questions and placing the monkey on a shoulder where it belongs, preferably not on the CECO's shoulder but rather on the CEO or someone in his executive team.

The interaction with executive management should be formalised to ensure continuity and consistency. We have seen various set-ups of how to structure this. A CECO does not necessarily have to be a member of the CEO's executive team but a firm tone from the top include giving the CECO necessary airtime at the executive management meetings. We recommend establishing an ethics committee (or similar), consisting of a sub-set of some executive management members; however, the issue with this set-up is that the executive

Monkey on the loose!

management team members will have different levels of knowledge regarding the issues, and in these sub-set committee meetings, the CEO may rarely be present. There are different ways of solving these issues, one way is to set up the ethics committee with some managers, such as from the support functions as permanent members of the committee and with managers from the operations who circulate annually. We have also seen organisations where the full executive team participates in specific compliance meetings which are separate from the ordinary leadership meetings in order to address the compliance topics. The risk here is that the tone from the top becomes weaker and weaker as the executive management team members begin to send in "substitutes" to the compliance meetings. Another set-up, which in our view can be very valuable, is when the monthly face-to-face executive management meeting always begins with a "code of conduct" agenda item. Begins. Not ends, in which case the agenda item risks falling off the table due to time constraints. When the work matures, it is natural to form ethics committees at the business area and unit levels within the organisation as well. One has to find a governance model that is aligned with the general governance structure of the company. Transparent discussion of cases coming in, investigations, the business culture and efforts to improve are vital and must, in one way or another, engage the full executive management team.

Monitoring

Monitoring efforts should, to as large an extent as possible, be integrated into the regular management control mechanisms of the company. To build an ethics and compliance programme is to build an "internal control framework" for aspects relating to conduct risks and how we do business, rather than the outcome (as the financial internal control framework relates to). If the company's internal control framework is mature, you should be able to design controls for, for example, the due diligence of third parties, your customer screenings, follow-up of sponsorships and donations and clean-up of customer data. If these control points are integrated into the existing control framework, you can add them to system support and external auditing procedures. Currently, the management and internal control frameworks focus a lot on the financial aspects of the business; this is a legacy from huge financial scandals such as the Enron and World-Com scandals in the beginning of the 21st century, when regulatory requirements were put on companies for adequate control over their financial reporting. Eventually, there will be regulatory requirements for companies to have adequate control over their "non-financial" reporting (such as sustainability or corporate responsibility reporting) as our scandals today reveal that the efforts to manage conduct risks described in annual and quarterly reports do not necessarily correspond to reality. Many companies are moving towards "integrated reporting", and this movement towards a more integrated approach to business and value creation/deterioration will require additional controls for how the company manages conduct risks.

We have worked with internal audits to define the scopes of audits that relate to a responsible business methodology and in their audits, they have found gaps and pressure points, enabling us to improve and get actions up on the table, in case they have been slipping. We have also at times worked with external compliance specialists to understand weaknesses and to help us prioritise better during the implementation of the programmes. There are also institutes and corporations that can evaluate and benchmark compliance programmes to give you feedback on where you stand in relation to others. These are examples of what you can do to test your programmes and get new lists of actions and priorities to work with. What is most important is that the effectiveness of the work is measured. Is the program evolving with the company? Is it working? Do you measure activities or do you measure whether these activities have an actual impact?

A few examples of questions a monitor might ask

Risk assessments: What different assessments and methods have been used to assess conduct risks? Have you had potential risks become manifested risks?

Organisation: How is the compliance function remunerated relevant to other executive positions? Has there been a turnover in the function? What are the experiences and education levels of the E&C team? Does the CECO have a relevant and independent budget?

Policies and Procedures: What is the process and who is included in designing policies and instructions? How are they made accessible?

Training and Communication: Do you have different training modules for different audiences? Do you use internal experiences of misconduct and dilemmas in the training? Have you ever checked if the training works and if so how?

Speak Up and Investigation: Who conducts investigations and what qualifications do these persons have? Do you frequently use external resources for investigations? Does the board or one of its sub-committees have full independent access to the investigations and results?

Remediation, Disciplinary and Corrective actions: How do you identify the root cause in investigations and how is this reflected in remediation efforts? How do you incentivise ethical behaviour?

Third parties: How is the third party conduct risk process structured? What control points do you use? How do you handle red flags? What does the escalation process look like? Do you monitor and follow-up on third parties?

Leadership: How is leadership trained on business ethics and culture? How does leadership express support for the E&C function and programmes?

Oversight, monitoring, governance: Does the internal audit conduct audits on conduct risks and culture? How are difficult decisions escalated? Who can decide on exceptions from the policy and rules?

Governance

How has the company ensured that it has operated consistently with regards to ethics and compliance e.g. the set internal control or policy framework? How do you ensure that the policies and procedures are implemented in subsidiaries and joint ventures? Is it clear that any group policy should and is implemented in a subsidiary or joint venture and how this process should be managed? Or does the topic have to be separately assessed for each subsidiary and joint venture? Our experience is that the board and shareholders, who read the annual reports on governance, risk and compliance, assume that the same principles apply for subsidiaries and joint ventures. Nevertheless, it seems like quite some fray and friction is involved to ensure that the subsidiary and joint venture boards actually adopt the policies, and also initiate, follow-up and measure implementation efforts. If the joint venture agreement does not include clauses on more specific actions for conduct risk, it can be very hard to implement an ethics and compliance programme in retrospect. Even if the subsidiary or joint venture board ratifies, for example, the anti-bribery corruption policy, it is just the beginning of the work (as you probably know by now having read a great part of this book). We suggest that your company should have clear principles for when the company policy framework must be applied, including principles on how to manage minority owned companies.

Executives quit after damning report into VimpelCom stake

Telecom group's finance director and general counsel resign over handling of its shareholding

Telenor's finance director and general counsel have resigned following the release of a damning external report into the handling of its stake in a Russian rival that has admitted corruption. A review by Deloitte, the professional services firm, found weaknesses in the Norwegian telecom group's structure, communications and leadership. The review focused on Telenor's handling of the 33 per cent shareholding in VimpelCom, particularly in relation to corruption allegations. [...] The corruption scandal has sullied Telenor's reputation and has led to changes to its board and executives. On Friday, [...] chief financial officer, and [...], general counsel, who had already been suspended, resigned. [...], Telenor's former chairman, was ousted in October after falling out with Norway's industry minister. Norway's

In a subsidiary, where the company have a majority stake, there are, in our view, no excuses for not implementing the same ethics and compliance programmes as for the wholly owned companies. There may be perfectly good reasons for avoiding too much central control from "the ivory tower", but the structures of governance in the group must ensure that all elements of the ethics and compliance programme are implemented to ensure adequate procedures and effective compliance throughout the entire group. When structuring the governance, it is important to keep in mind that certain decisions, for example, to turn down direct requests from local customers or officials, can be very hard to do locally. To ease the pressure from local colleagues, we recommend that the escalation process for some decisions "jump the hierarchy", such as, for example, whether to use a particular supplier, agent or make certain donations, from local to regional to global to enable strong decisions on difficult dilemmas. Some decisions are just too sensitive to make at a local or even regional level and must therefore be escalated to avoid pressure internally or externally. Escalations on disciplinary and corrective actions must always "jump the hierarchy" to avoid conflict of interest, in a situation where a local CEO shall decide on actions related to wrongdoing by one of his direct reports. The structure and instructions of the local, regional and global ethics committees should set out how and when matters are escalated to the next level.

We argue that sometimes decentralisation is in fact more than only ensuring local accountability and autonomy; rather, it is driven by an urge to push difficult and uncomfortable situations away from the top and create a false sense of security. A dedicated ethics and compliance officer who visits remote locations may be surprised by how little executive management is aware of how things actually are done on the ground. They see the sales figures and may know the important customers, but have no clue of the difficult dilemmas that the local colleagues are facing to secure that sale and win those customers. The task of the ethics and compliance team is to bridge this gap; to support the local colleagues to do things right and support executive management with information to ensure they are aware of the risks and dilemmas and can manage and resolve these in the right way.

The role of the General Counsel

Many governance models describe the general counsel (GC) as an extra safety to the boards, assuming that the GC will escalate relevant concerns to them. I take issue with this notion. Having worked as a corporate lawyer and a GC in many companies, I am certain that yes, you can use that escalation opportunity, but only once. Then, you will have destroyed any good relationship you have built with the CEO and the executive management. The board need to understand that when push comes to shove, the GC is really the CEOs counsel and that few like to be by-passed and somewhat lose control over the board. There are many excellent GCs with high integrity and capacity to walk the tightrope between the board and the executive management. However, boards should not assume that these champion GCs work in their companies and might instead consider establishing firmer lines of independent reporting and information to internal audit and the ethics and compliance function to ensure that they have relevant information to govern the company.

Oversight, monitoring and governance – a quick checklist

- ✓ At the highest level, oversight is exercised at board level. Does the CECO have access to the board? Does the CECO have access to the CEO and the executive management?

- ✓ Friction and intolerance of friction is the biggest challenge to the ethics and compliance programmes. Are the board and management aware?

- ✓ Internal Audit, external audits or an external monitor can help test the programmes to identify weaknesses and areas of improvement.

- ✓ How are the affiliates and subsidiaries governed?

- ✓ How are the ethics and compliance programmes governed?

CHAPTER SIX

Conduct and Culture – From Action to Change

Working with corporate conduct is working with change. Even if we all claim to embrace change, we know that change is hard and that it requires time and patience. There will inevitably be resistance to change and to the compliance programmes. Some colleagues will support the efforts and welcome the initiatives, while others will remain unconvinced and perhaps doubt if it really concerns them or if it is even possible. Some will be insulted and provoked by statements of "change", "ethics" and "responsibility", statements implying that they have not done their job properly before. Sometimes the company is in a situation where there is less urgency, there is time and you can be patient. Sometimes the company is in a situation where there is urgency, a public scandal or looming criminal investigations, and you have no time and no patience. Resistance is easier to deal with when you have calm waters than when there is a full storm, which in itself creates additional friction and discomfort. Some of this resistance may be vocal and direct and easier to deal with, but some resistance is voiced behind closed doors and behind your back: "silent resistance". The silent resistance may take a break when the crisis is ongoing, and it may even go away as more and more people embrace change, but some resistance remains and will pop up and take action when the opportunity arises, undermining the effectiveness of the programme and the journey towards a renewed culture and change. Change creates friction, and change requires a strong and sound "tone from the top".

Leadership and the real "tone from the top"

The phrase "tone from the top" is frequently used to describe support and direction from top management. Tone from the top is a basic requirement of effective compliance. But what does it really mean? Some years back, the "top" in the company – the board, the CEO and executive management – could perhaps get away with a statement of support, with typical words such as "we have zero tolerance for corruption" or "we feel strongly about human rights". While statements are necessary, we know today that more is required from "the top" than words. Especially as bonus schemes and evaluation models oftentimes are contradictory and drive unwanted conduct, ensuring short-term sales or financial results. For example, when the sales bonuses of a regional manager and her or his team are tied to deals with a particular important regional customer and a local intermediary traditionally facilitates these deals. The risks of bribery using a local intermediary are very high, but for the regional manager must be weighed against the risk of a lost deal and with it, a large part of her or his annual compensation. Better understanding of underlying tensions can ensure that incentive systems are built to encourage the right decisions and saying no to risky deals.

Instead of "a tone", we view "tone from the top" as leadership. Leadership at all levels, assuming responsibility not only for *what* the company does but also for *how* it is done. Leadership, demonstrated in decisions made and decisions refrained from. Leadership that is present when misconduct is detected and it is time for disciplinary actions. Through decisions and actions, leadership can promote or hinder change. The ethics and compliance team can implement the elements of compliance, do risk assessments, training and screening of third parties, but cannot and should not make the crucial decisions. Structures that facilitate flow of information, discussions, transparency and escalation when necessary will form the basis, but corporate conduct is ultimately about individuals making the right decisions and doing the right things. The ethics and compliance team can lead the horse to water but cannot make it drink.

Leadership is when top management and the board understand the existence and the consequences of "friction and dilemmas", which is the result of effective compliance work. The ethics and compliance team are experts in identifying, assessing and proposing mitigating actions for conduct-related risks, but management is responsible for the decisions and implementation. It is tempting to outsource responsibility for the "compliance risk" (for example, if using a particular sales intermediary is okay or not) to the ethics and compliance team, but the "compliance risk" (in this case a legal, ethical, reputational and human rights risk of bribery) must be part of the business decision. The ethics and compliance team should not make decisions for management but can guide, advise and assist – and escalate in case of misalignment. Good governance does not entail delegating responsibility for decisions to the ethics and compliance team "I am okay with this, providing that the E&C people are okay" does not fit in a delegation of authority matrix. This approach makes visible a lack of management ownership and ultimately signals poor leadership and very weak tone from the top.

Some examples of a broken tone

• A sales manager is always travelling in business class when the company policy states that economy class is to be used for corporate travels. In addition, the sales manager is known for inviting "sales contacts" and their families to expensive restaurants. Senior management is aware of the issues but is not reacting as the sales manager is very successful and brings in increasing revenues.

• The company has performed a supplier audit on a critical supplier in Bangladesh. During the site visit it becomes obvious that the supplier has no relevant tools or rules for health and safety and for ensuring decent working hours, which is a breach of the Supplier / Business Partner Code of Conduct. The local sourcing manager proposes a development plan for the local supplier, including a request for additional resources to secure implementation of this development plan. Her boss, the global sourcing manager, escalates the issues and need for additional resources to the sourcing committee. The sourcing committee acknowledge the issues but conclude that no additional resources can be allocated to secure compliance as the margins already are thin and the supplier was selected based on best price criteria.

- The company has a subsidiary in Kyrgyzstan. Last year the local subsidiary received a request, from the government department of technology, to sponsor a countrywide project for children to improve their internet skills. According to the donations policy a governmental request must be assessed by ethics and compliance and the donation was approved on the condition that there is transparency into how the funds are used. The next year the local CEO receives a similar donation request and as no reports or accounts have been received for the previous project, the ethics and compliance team advise the local CEO to refrain from paying and to engage in a dialogue with the department of technology. The local CEO escalates the issue to the Government Relations Officer and explains that the local subsidiary will suffer going forwards in all its important dealings with the government if they do not pay. During a compliance visit a few months later the ethics and compliance team learn that the Government Relations Officer has approved the request.

- The company has won a big construction deal in Peru, its first in South America so it is a rather important deal. It turns out that to get the contract signed and start the work, the company needs to engage a local agent who will mediate between the government and the company throughout the construction. The agent shall be paid 4 % of the contract amount. The due diligence report concludes critical findings, as it is unclear who is the ultimate beneficiary of the agent and why the government has selected this particular agent. The ethics and compliance team advise a no-go before clarity into the UBO has been established. The local CEO has arranged for a local legal opinion relating to the use of the agent and propose to the business management to proceed.

- The company is appointing a new external board member for one of its subsidiaries. The due diligence report states that the prospective board member has been engaged in a company that has filed for bankruptcy and among the debts are large tax debts along with other less prioritised debt. The local HR manager is somewhat concerned as she has understood from articles in newspapers recently that tax planning and tax debts can be a reputational liability. She escalates the due diligence findings to the regional HR manager. The regional HR manager dismisses her concerns with a laugh and tells her that it is ridiculous to discuss such issues.

The manner in which these and other dilemmas are resolved will build the company culture. Every decision and every action counts. Most of us know IKEA, the department store with everything and anything for your home, with furniture sold at very competitive prices and a heaven for the DIY fanatic. Rumour has it that the founder and owner of IKEA, Ingvar Kamprad, refused to travel business class and drove a shabby old car to reinforce his view on corporate travel and spending. Leaders are role models, and Kamprad was extremely successful in setting a tone of frugality in IKEA. People look very carefully at what leaders do. The CEO dresses in light blue shirts without a tie, and sure enough pretty soon, all the men in the leadership team wear shirts without ties and soon also their next layer of male reports. What happens then, if the head of sales always orders the most expensive bottle of wine during a business dinner? What if the general counsel gossips with her or his subordinates about colleagues in the leadership team? What if the CEO humiliates people who get things wrong?

The "tone from the top" is not just set at the very "top", the executive management and the board. A direction is set at the top but to mean something, the direction must be reinforced and confirmed at all levels of management in the company. But do not despair if the tone from the top is weak at times. There are many important leaders in the organisation who can be front-runners and supporters of ethical business. Their words, actions and decisions will certainly build a culture around them and in their teams. The ethics and compliance team can support these teams and by joining forces, a momentum will build towards broader change. All leaders and employees are important to build a culture of business ethics and compliance, and the compliance programme is also reinforced from the bottom up.

Friction as a driver for change

By implementing the framework for corporate conduct, you will have the opportunity to build a transparent and ethical culture and ultimately a better and more sustainable company. But it is not a walk in the park. In our work with implementing ethics and compliance, it has become very evident that, at times, it can become quite uncomfortable when dilemmas, ethical struggles and friction generate discomfort and personal priorities surface. well-designed compliance programme will generate friction, will reveal conflicting priorities and will test if the company is willing to truly live by the Code of Conduct and its claimed values. It is difficult to agree on and come to easy decisions when a big sales deal is at stake or an acquisition is in the making. To move from words into action, ensuring that the compliance efforts lead to actual change, the situations of friction need to be approached with leadership, courage and transparency. Words do not create culture, action does. And friction is a sign of action.

Friction is a sign of action.

Through escalation processes, managers who previously may have been sheltered from the issues, ignored them or pushed them back downwards in the organisation, find themselves in uncharted waters. Difficult dilemmas, conflicting priorities and "known-but-silenced-violations" are exposed and laid bare. Irritation and frustration replace previous comfortable feelings of unity and collegiality. This is not very nice, but it is necessary. By pushing through this friction and by resolving the dilemmas with respect and persistence, the culture will be built and refined and will ultimately build a stronger and more transparent company. It is perhaps more natural to resist and ignore friction and dilemmas than to embrace and deal with them. The ethics and compliance team may themselves be perceived as difficult when the programme, through training, escalation procedures, investigations and remedial actions, forces the difficult dilemmas upwards in the organisation.

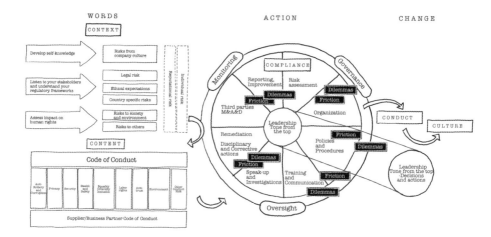

The *Friction* and *Dilemmas* are evidence of effective compliance work and create requirements for *Decisions* and *Actions* for *Conduct*. Repeated and consistent *Conduct* creates *Culture*.

A strong culture of business ethics supports the implementation of the framework; strong common values such as honesty, integrity, diversity, openness, fairness, trust, non-discrimination and non-retaliation will make it easier to cope with the friction and the dilemmas. A strong culture is fostered as the organisation gets used to the transparency, to the push of the ethics and compliance programmes and to the "new" information, priorities and visibility. By training the leaders in ethical awareness and in the choices that they have, it will become easier and easier to understand and deal with the friction. A sudden decrease in friction and dilemmas, on the other hand, can also be a disturbing sign of stagnation or resistance. The "unwanted information" is instead removed or reduced through layers of organisational filter. Alternatively, the decrease in friction may be a sign of an oppressive culture, which does not allow for constructive dialogue around the dilemmas, choices and subsequent decisions.

How to manage friction and dilemmas

While implementing effective compliance, we have experienced friction when it comes to resources and prioritisation, on red flags and inferences, on acknowledging the problem, on transparency or turning a blind eye, on disciplinary actions and on sales incentives. On settling for legal compliance or ethical standards, shall we do what we can get away with, shall we hide behind "not knowing" or shall we hope that "no one finds out"? Many have been annoyed with us for bringing the issues to the table; we have been annoyed with many for downplaying the issues and ignoring patterns of risky behaviour and critical red flags.

We have felt misunderstood; we are nice people but it is our job to problematise, bring up the difficult matters and demand decisions at the relevant level of responsibility and authority in the company – to protect the company and its stakeholders. Managers have felt misunderstood and pressured from different angles – to do the right thing is sometimes hard – should you show good or at least presentable quarterly results or pause and clean up historical issues?

> **It is our job to problematise, bring up the difficult matters and demand decisions at the relevant level of responsibility and authority in the company.**

Can you do both with limited resources and time?

Sometimes you find yourself stuck between a rock and a hard place. As a business lawyer, you are trained to "support the business", meaning never saying no or being difficult but to find solutions or "workarounds". As an ethics and compliance professional, "no" may be the only right answer and "workarounds" is not in your vocabulary. As a finance manager, your main job is to "stick to the budget" and as a sales manager "to get the sales", thus, saying "no" may mean that the budget is ruined and the sales are lost. As ethics and compliance professionals, we truly believe that the work to make the ethical dilemmas visible is in the best interest of the company, its leaders, its decision makers and its owners. However, instead you may be viewed as not being a "team player". Faced with critical dilemmas and struggles, you may worry about your personal responsibilities – can we be held accountable if we do not have the power to act? Working together, facing the struggles and friction, feeling the tension, irritation and dislike, at one point in time, we told each other that we are doing something wrong as this is not working … but then we realised … this is how it is when it is working! All the arguments and all the discussions were signs that something was happening. We started to see that all the drama was evidence that the compliance efforts were working and we understood that instead of fighting the friction, we should relate to the friction as a change agent. We understood that the friction should be viewed as energy, as fuel to the change, and as a sign of action and a reason to keep calm and carry on. The friction and dilemmas created a need for escalation processes and courageous leadership, a need for firm decisions and clear actions. We realised that a better understanding of how friction, discomfort and other human factors influence us and sometimes prevent us from making the right choices is paramount if a company wants to develop the corporate culture of business ethics. Supporting and training leaders in aspects of friction is, in our view, a vital component of ethics and compliance work. Friction is not something that anyone strives for, but it is a pre-requisite for change of conduct. When faced with friction and struggles, see the friction as proof that the programme is actually working; see it as an opportunity to build and enforce the culture.

Friction is the most important reason for owners and boards to consider reporting lines, autonomy and a certain protection of the ethics and compliance organisation. Because of the friction and the filters built into any organisational structure, the CECO should have direct access to the board or one of its subcommittees. This reporting line ensures independence of the ethics and compliance function and commitment from the very top and is a practical and efficient manner of ensuring that board members also develop competence in the area of conduct risks, business ethics and stakeholder interests.

There are companies with longstanding histories of working with ethics and compliance, supported by good values and strong, sound corporate culture. In these companies, the friction will not be that overwhelming, as the culture will support resolving the dilemmas as part of the daily work. Other companies are in the midst of a major scandal and have deep problems with both culture and compliance. In these companies, there will inevitably be more friction and many difficult dilemmas, but hopefully, as the programmes progress, awareness builds and dilemmas are satisfactorily solved, the culture matures. If the friction is not managed, the dilemmas pushed away and/or solved without understanding the root causes, the culture will not change. The company will not truly transform and the never-easing prevalence of friction will break both people and structures.

Ethical blind spots and why good people make bad decisions

The theory of ethical blindness, developed by Professor Guido Palazzo, shows how the context and situation can put you in a situation where you run a high risk of making wrong decisions or doing things you normally would not do. When the pressure is lifted, you may not understand how you could end up being so wrong or acting as you did. Fear, group pressures, time pressure, distancing yourself from the discomfort of witnessing other people's suffering, or to the ultimate consequences of your actions all contribute to ethical blindness. Some decisions become normal in a particular setting and context but are viewed as abnormal in another. Ethical blindness and normalisation can be the result of organisational structure or corporate culture; the company itself becomes a "tunnel of fear", preventing you from seeing outside of the tunnel. Elements such as unrealistic targets, humiliating performance evaluations, ambivalent messages such as "do the right thing – but make sure to seal the deal at any cost" and aggressive language such as "this is a life and death deal" and "we are at war with the competition" all feed ethical blindness and normalisation. Another factor is "delegating compliance" too low in the organisation. Even if we advocate that ethics and compliance is an individual respon-sibility of all employees, a global company cannot assume that a local finance or sales manager in, for example, Angola or Mexico, alone can manage the risks of corruption. The head office cannot only issue a policy, launch a mandatory e-learning course and state "zero tolerance for corruption" and assume that employees facing continuous requests for bribes and corruption do not need any more support. They do. "Fix the problem – don't come to me with issues" is thus another pitfall.

We have found it very rewarding to talk about ethical blindness and normalisation in our training, not in the interests of justifying or "forgiving" wrongdoings but with the purpose of raising aware-ness of the complexities of "doing the right thing".

In discussions on ethical blindness, we quite often hear reference to "the rogue employee" or "the bad apple". A company that has ended up in a crisis or conduct failure explains that the problem is fixed, as they have fired the responsible employee – "the bad apple". Our experience is however that this is rarely the case; the core problem is not fixed. Quite the opposite, more often, a conduct failure is not the fault of only one individual but a sign that there may be broader, perhaps systemic, issues with a non-transparent and problematic culture.

Normalisation and ethical blindness make life in the grey zone more difficult; we are lured into patterns, behaviour, inertia and inaction while totally unaware it is happening. It is just normal and we do not react until something triggers us to look at the phenomena with different glasses. We walk around in cities with big billboards, advertising fashion with young girls in very compromising positions, half-naked with a chain around their necks. We go to the big car-show in Geneva and cars are displayed with young girls in bikinis plastered over the engine hood. What the #metoo movement has brought to the surface is that we have been so used to lewd jokes, foul language and business entertainment involving escort services and visits to strip clubs that we have not reacted. Corruption is another example where the unwanted has become normal. In many societies, people have just accepted that corruption is part of their daily life, it has always been so and they are used to finding ways to work the system. Very few in a corrupt society deem corruption as right and good, as it is not only wrong but also detrimental to their daily life, existence and society, but they are so used to it that corruption has become normal. Until very recently, we did not seem to react to the fact that the property market in London and other big cosmopolitan cities are like washing machines for corrupt money and that tax havens are used for more than just tax optimisation but actually enable concealing stolen wealth on small islands in the Channel, Mediterranean or Caribbean. Another example of normalisation is the fiddling with emissions tests at Volkswagen. A few engineers became scapegoats and were fired, while it seems rather obvious that fiddling with the levels of emissions in test environments was a normal manner of "working around the problem", possibly not only at VW but in the whole automotive industry.

Asch's experiment on group pressure

Initially conducted quite a long time ago, in the early 1950s, Asch used a group of eight male students who participated in a simple "perception task". In fact, all persons in the test were actors, except one who unknowingly was the real target of the study. All students were shown two cards: one card with one line and one card with three lines – A, B and C.

In summary of Asch's conformity experiments and theory,[29] the students were asked to think over the two cards and answer which one of the three lines A, B or C on the card to the right they thought were as high as the one line on the card to the left. In a situation where all seven "actor-students" answered the same incorrect answer (A or C instead of the obvious B), the real eighth student conformed with the others two-thirds of the time.

Exposed to group pressure, we tend to conform, not because we necessarily can identify the pressure and lazily "go along with the rest" but more often, because we become insecure and unsure and think that something is wrong with us or we have somehow misunderstood the task.

Equality, diversity and inclusion

A diverse, equal and inclusive workplace is better equipped to manage and deal with differences, including differences of opinion. Friction is practised on an everyday basis when more opinions are invited to the table and you learn to see things from a new angle. Inclusion invites authenticity, openness and curiosity as well as respect, and the culture this brings is helpful when friction from conduct-related matters surfaces and must be managed. In a Harvard Business Review article,[30] we can read about why diverse

29   https://www.simplypsychology.org/asch-conformity.html
30   https://hbr.org/2016/11/why-diverse-teams-are-smarter

management teams are smarter. The article states, "Diverse teams are more likely to constantly reexamine facts and remain objective. They may also encourage greater scrutiny of each member's actions, keeping their joint cognitive resources sharp and vigilant.

By breaking up workplace homogeneity, you can allow your employees to become more aware of their own potential biases – entrenched ways of

Diverse management teams are smarter

thinking that can otherwise blind them to key information and even lead them to make errors in decision-making processes". We believe that diverse, inclusive management teams are also better equipped to manage conduct risk and that homogeneity in teams can be a lurking risk. And in the aftermaths of #metoo movement, we know that there still is a lot of improvement needed within the area of discrimination, diversity and equality.

Safety, Diversity and Inclusion

A Swedish construction company with high requirements for safety at work, has conducted a study to see how diversity and inclusion interrelate and affect safety. They concluded that a high level of diversity but with a low level of inclusion (typically a very hierarchical workplace, where non-transparent decisions are made at the top) creates an environment with low work-satisfaction, high employee turnover, weak employer brand and low creativity and innovation but also a low level of safety. On the other hand, a high level of inclusion but with low diversity (typically a company, where the decisions are thoroughly discussed and shared e.g. "the Swedish model"

but with very homogenous power structures) creates a work environment with a high employee satisfaction but too low employee turnover, a strong but narrow employee brand, low creativity and innovation and high risk for "group-think" but also a low to medium level of safety. Not so surprising, the company concluded that a combination of high diversity and high inclusion created a workplace with high level of employee satisfaction, healthy employee turnover, a strong employee brand, high creativity and innovation, high level of agility (open-minded atmosphere, where it is easy to make your voice heard) and – (yes!) – a much better safety record.

Silence is not golden

Many corporate scandals originate from media reports when investigative journalists reveal failures in corporate conduct. Many legal processes are initiated as a consequence of these external media reports. Even if it may be tempting to blame the media or journalists, it is not the media coverage or the prosecutor that has caused the scandal in the first place. The scandal originates from within. More often than not, there are employees who tried to raise their voices and point out that something must be wrong. Too often, nobody wanted to listen to them, their concerns were taken lightly, and they were perhaps called "trouble makers", "nay-sayers", "negative and difficult" and "un-collegial". These employees were perhaps not only ignored but some were even demoted or fired. Many corporate scandals originate from a disgruntled employee, a silenced messenger that has reached out externally. We see this over and over again, where the scandal starts from within, by ignoring voices of reason.

CASE Olympus Scandal

On 14 October 2011, after a mere 6 months as the President and two weeks as CEO of Olympus Corporation, Michael Woodford was suddenly fired. An article in a Japanese magazine prompted his attention and he soon uncovered irregularities in accounting and realised that the company had systematically covered up losses. When he brought the matter to the board, instead of praise for his diligence he was fired. The incident rapidly became a huge scandal and crisis in Olympus with falling share price, prosecutions and reputational loss. Michael Woodford has written a book called "Exposure" about his experience working in a company he loved, being promoted and proud, how he almost reluctantly started and continued investigating the allegations in the article until he found them substantiated. How he tried in vain to raise his concerns with the board, owners and auditors, and was subsequently fired, threatened and chased out of Japan and how he fought back. It is a great book, a thriller from real corporate life.

Crisis as a pre-requisite for change

Is it necessary with a [conduct-] crisis to bring attention to ethics and compliance? We get asked this question very often. The answer is usually "no, but it helps … initially". At the outset, the crisis makes everyone aware and willing to spend time and money on ethics and compliance, as a need for change in conduct, culture and leadership is obvious. However, any crisis is tiring for the management and the employees, and a crisis that lasts for years is exhausting and steals time and focus away from daily business operations. In a prolonged crisis, the company may become a symbol for crisis and there will be a strong urge to rid oneself of the past and the tainted affair. There will be talk of "focusing on the business", as if controls, assurance, compliance and responsibility are not one with the business but an extra or side matter that you do when you can afford it or when you are forced to due to circumstances. It is understandable that friction created by the implementation of the ethics and compliance programme wears people down, a normal but unfortunate effect of crisis, and well known among those who are experienced in working in crisis situations. However, compliance is not crisis management; it is a methodology to ensure that what is said is also done. A methodology to ensure that identified conduct risks are mitigated and managed. It is a strong fundamental enabler in building the culture, and it should not go away when the crisis subsides. On the contrary, the company should use its substantial experience, drawn from the crisis and all the related hard work, to strengthen its values, operations and business.

When accused of ethical misconduct, we commonly read that the company has "intensified its ethics and compliance work". Companies tend to act reactively, but times are changing; we see more companies setting up solid ethics and compliance functions without a crisis forcing them to do so. If you work in a company without a raging crisis, you may feel a need to create a sense of urgency to get management's attention and to avoid complacency. You may feel a need to create your own little "mini-crisis". We have seen that you can elevate the awareness and get management's attention in various ways. Make solid assessments of the context and countries in which you operate, do in-depth analysis of your whistle-blowing cases, look at where other companies have ended up in trouble and conduct risk assessments to understand whether you may have these same issues in your company. If you have read about a company getting into trouble for an agent in India, camouflaged as a "technical consultant", look at the third parties involved in your Indian sales operations. If you read about a competitor struggling with fraud relating to particular subcontracting work, look through your projects and subcontractors as well. Probably these are not isolated events, only occurring outside your own company. It is a changed world and we are certain that any company, operating on a global scale, have their fair share of challenges. What we see in the open, the scandals and the headlines, is only the tip of the iceberg. Most companies have an opportunity to clean up their house and ensure effective compliance and adequate procedures without an external / public crisis. Forewarned is certainly forearmed, should media/reputational crisis or law enforcement strike. Be your own investigative journalist, make sure to use the time wisely, as one CEO said "it is not a matter of if – it is a matter of when". Most CEOs know there are skeletons in their closets, and by being proactive there is a great opportunity to make things right.

Accepting friction

When we speak about friction with our colleagues in the ethics and compliance profession, we often get an immediate reaction of recognition and relief: "it's not just me – I am not going crazy". It is hard to have a profession where your job is to be uncomfortable, it is tempting to indulge in self-pity and complain that no one understands you. To understand the friction, to have a model of explanation of the friction, helps you to distance yourself from it and to look at it a little bit more objectively – it certainly has helped us. Understanding the friction also helps you understand and empathize with leadership: it is not easy to be the one who ultimately has to make the difficult decisions, the one who meets their bosses, boards, shareholders and considers different, sometimes conflicting, priorities and demands. Everyone benefits from understanding how we normally react to friction; some people are rather good at handling the fray and friction and some are inexperienced and get more easily exhausted and offended. Some shy away from friction and disagreement and seek consensus by ignoring different opinions or choosing to work with people who are like-minded and who make you feel good about yourself.

Understanding structures designed to shelter managers from friction is vital. A delegated governance structure, where responsibility and accountability for the operations are delegated to local management and local boards can feel quite comfortable when you are an executive manager or board member at group level. However, this model can be dangerous from a conduct perspective, when problems emerge locally. In some cases, this governance structure can protect the global management and board from personal legal liability, but it is rather useless as protection when it comes to reputational risks as well ethical expectations risk and societal risk. And increasingly we see the CEO and the board of directors being held accountable for "not knowing". In addition, some conduct-related friction and dilemmas are not possible to resolve in a satisfactory manner locally, as the problem causing the friction lies in the external context of the local business, such as corruption and kleptocracy. Make sure to implement formal governance structures to escalate the dilemmas to appropriate levels of management in operational processes such as sourcing, contract management and approvals. Despite the additional friction involved, clear escalation procedures for conduct-related matters are needed to avoid conduct failures and maintain some control and oversight on how the local company is operating, not only in the "what", which normally is very closely monitored through the financial reporting systems but also in the "how".

One manner of understanding and managing friction and difficult dilemmas is using "legal opinions", advice from prominent [and expensive] law firms on the legal aspects of the dilemma. The legal aspects are certainly important and relevant but sometimes not exhaustive, as a legal opinion may not take into consideration reputational damage, failure to live up to ethical expectations or societal risk. In some cases, a legal opinion will not even protect the company or its directors from legal responsibility as we can see in, for example, the VimpelCom case. In some jurisdictions, the legal process is corrupt, ineffective or just slow and drawn out so that by the time you have the ultimate answer as to whether a conduct is legal or not, the ship has sailed and the damage is already done. Increasingly, we see how other extraterritorial jurisdictions move in where the "home" judiciary system has failed.

Legal opinions and the Vimpelcom bribery scandal

In February 2016, Vimpelcom (subsequently rebranded Veon) reached a settlement with the US Department of Justice, Securities and Exchange Commission and prosecutor, acknowledging bribery and kleptocracy under the US FCPA and Dutch laws. From the settlement documents, we can read that there was a "witness" within the Vimpelcom organisation that years earlier had escalated concerns regarding bribery and corruption. The Board of Vimpelcom asked for a legal opinion to ascertain compliance with FCPA. The Board was subsequently presented with two legal opinions, which did not stop the Board from approving the Joint Venture setup in Uzbekistan. The legal opinion was probably, at the time, not wrong per se, it just did not consider all aspects of jurisdictional reach, ethical expectations and reputational risks. Maybe the scope of the legal opinion was described too narrowly by the company or maybe the Board was not presented with all the disclaimers and recommendations in the opinion. In any case, the legal opinion did not, as events unfolded some ten years after, protect the company nor its directors.

Some lawyers have the integrity and confidence to write legal opinions that take into consideration the fact that laws are often not a black and white situation, including also risks of ethical expectations, societal risk and reputation. In contrast, other lawyers are very confident that their interpretation of law is correct and clear cut and that aspects of ethics, reputation and societal risks are not within the scope of the legal opinion and their responsibility. Consequently, any legal opinion must be viewed as one aspect to consider among many in deciding on difficult dilemmas, and does not absolve you from the requirement to form your own opinion.

Culture is what you do - in the grey zone!

So, if the legal opinion is only partially helpful, maybe a more rigorous view on compliance can protect the organisation from conduct failures? Maybe additional controls and added policies and procedures will provide an "illuminated highway" for decision-making? When is it clear what is right and what is wrong, how can you remove uncertainty and establish a line between black and white? Well, we hate to break the news, but it is not that simple as global business is also not that simple. The corner stones of effective compliance are the groundwork, the platform and the tools to get the dilemmas out in the open and generate the need for transparent decisions and action. Forcing the choices out into the open – a space we call the grey zone – enables leaders and employees to make informed decisions. It is what happens in the grey zone that defines the company and where the conduct will create or reinforce the corporate culture. Being a leader is never easy and leaders may long for affirmative advice on black or white and sure, sometimes black is black and white is white, but more often it is grey and a matter of judging priorities and risks, ethics and responsibility. On top of the uncertainty, you add the discomfort brought on by transparency and the friction, which is the result of effective compliance work. Life in the grey zone is certainly neither easy nor comfortable. Neither is it taught at business schools or law faculties. The world today is increasingly complex, increasingly grey and increasingly demanding with requirements of transparency, which, in the end, may be the only way to protect yourself when making difficult decisions. Managing corporate conduct will always require navigating in the grey zone; thus, leaders and employees must train

and build this competence. Build the ethical core, exercise the ethical muscles, find the courage by practising resolving dilemmas and getting used to friction. For an ethics and compliance programme to be truly effective and successful, and to achieve a conduct that strengthens the corporate culture, we must address and support leadership in the grey zone.

Oftentimes, in the midst of a conduct failure made public, you will have calls for compliance and added layers of controls. Sometimes this is required as the organisation in question has not implemented the fundamental cornerstones of compliance and has inadequate control systems in place. But sometimes, even we, as ethics and compliance professionals, cringe as responsibilities and trust are taken away from leaders who are left feeling less and less empowered to think for themselves.

Doing business will always involve uncertainty, incomplete information, conflicting demands and changing requirements – a leader will always have to navigate in the grey zone. To be a leader is a tough job with many demands, not only to bring revenue and value to the company but also to ensure that the generated profits and value are not eroded by bad conduct, by disregarding or mismanaging risks. The bar is being raised all the time, what was ok yesterday may not be ok tomorrow. News, regardless of whether it is true or not, spreads globally at the speed of light. A leader should be a good role model, able to manage friction, make difficult decisions, have a solid ethical core held up by strong ethical muscles, be courageous and not push uncomfortable dilemmas aside. It helps if one also truly believes that an ethical and responsible business will build a better, stronger, sustainable company and a better, stronger and sustainable society and environment. Corporate conduct – compliance and business ethics – is ultimately a matter of responsible leadership, with genuine and brave leaders having a grounded understanding of

Ethics and Compliance, empowering businesses and their leaders

what a big role companies play in the world and having an optimistic view of what she/he and companies can accomplish if they set their hearts to it. Business leaders doing what they do best – leading and growing businesses – can change the way of the world.

We believe in business leaders and that they can be a catalyst for change and can be trusted to make the right decisions in the grey zone. We believe that this is possible through systematic work, by creating processes and governance structures that embrace friction and struggles and promote transparency and does not shy away

Ethics is the possibility, the capability and the courage to choose.

from difficult discussions. The framework for corporate conduct, described in this book, provides a tool for navigating in the grey zone and a means for facilitating change.